In religion, there are **seven** deadly sins that **every person** must deal with sooner or later:
Gluttony
Greed
Sloth
Pride
Envy
Wrath
Lust

In relationships, there are **five** deadly questions that **every guy** must deal with sooner or later:
Does this dress make my ass look fat?
How many women have you slept with?
Should I get a boob job?
Do you think I'd make a good prostitute?
How can I get her to sign the pre-nup?

Forget about Dr. Phil, Wayne, Laura, Dr. Ruth, and all of the other relationship gurus: read this book and learn how to maintain control of your own personal situation.

Dr. Nick Shoveen, Ph.D.

FEMALE-TO-ENGLISH DICTIONARY
(Abridged Edition)

An Annotated Guide to Interpreting & Manipulating Female Thought Processes

By Dr. Nick Shoveen, Ph.D.

Bonus Feature:
Discussion section on
Pre-nuptial Agreements

From Magic Lamp Press
Venice, California

If you purchased this book without a cover, you should be aware that this book is stolen property. It was reported 'unsold and destroyed' to the publisher and neither the author nor the publisher has received any payment for this "stripped book."

This is a work of fiction. Names, characters, places, and incidents are either the product of the author's imagination or are used fictitiously or with permission. Any resemblance to actual persons, living or dead, or any events, is entirely coincidental.

FEMALE-TO-ENGLISH DICTIONARY
(Abridged Edition)
An Annotated Guide to Interpreting & Manipulating Female Thought Processes

All rights reserved
© MMVI Magic Lamp Press

This book, or parts thereof, may not be reproduced in any form, stored in a retrieval system, or transmitted by any means, electronic, mechanical, photocopying, recording, or otherwise, without written permission from the author. For written permission, contact: Magic Lamp Press, P.O. Box 9547, Marina del Rey, CA 90295.

http://www.whatwomenreallymean.com

ISBN: 1-882629-11-6

Your Miranda Warning

As you probably know, females have an uncanny memory. They never forget a word you say. Everything you say can and will be used against you some time in the future.

The only way to combat this is with your own proper note taking. Whenever she says something you want to remember, make sure not only to write it down in this book, but also put in the date she said it. Then, when you bring something up to her that she said in the past, you can also tell her exactly what day she said it.

This will act to blow her mind, and give her the impression that you actually listen to what she says, even though it doesn't look like you do.

Another benefit to keeping notes in this book is that someday you can pass this book on to your son, so that he can have a chance in his relationships.

And, if your child is a daughter, you might consider breaking the rules and giving the book to her way before she grows up, so that she can avoid being manipulated by some guy like you.

Table of Contents

Introduction 1
Silence 6
Body Language 16
It's all done with Mirrors 20
Depreciation 24
It's Been a Long Time 30
Dirty Words 36
Humor Me 40
First Impressions 46
The Ultimatum Clock 56
Your New Life (what's left of it) 62
On a Clear Day 64
The WWW (World-Wide-Wait) 68
A Biscuit, a Basket 72
Miss Daisy, Driving 74
The Gift Horse 76
The Loneliest Number 78
MoveOn.Don't 82
Walk This Way 86
Curiosity Killed the Cat 90
Entrapment 94
Outside the Beltway 100
Internal Affairs 104
The Substitute? 108
A Blank Slate 114
Petty Theft 116
Have it Your Way 120

Wanderlust	124
It's on Sale	128
You Are What You Eat	132
The Bug	134
Tools of the Trade	138
Sacrifice Bunt	140
Lord of the Ring	142
Rules of Engagement	150
Back to Earth	154
The Party's Over	160
Suggestions for a Better World	164
Appendix: The Pre-Nuptial Agreement	170

> "Sometimes I wonder if men and women really suit each other. Perhaps they should live next door and just visit now and then."
>
> *Katherine Hepburn*

1

Introduction

When a male falls for a female, he likes how she looks and how she acts toward him, and he foolishly expects her to stay that way forever.

On the other hand, when a female finally decides to compromise her ideals and settle down with a male, she usually doesn't like what she sees. This isn't what she was always hoping for, her 'mister right.' That prince charming never rode into her life on his white horse. Instead, she gets a dose of reality and decides to accept what's available and willing, notwithstanding the fact that he probably

The Abridged Female-to-English Dictionary
by Dr. Nick Shoveen, Ph.D.

believes that the greatest invention since the beginning of time is the remote control.

Because you'll never be her dream-man personified, this poor male can never really measure up to what she was hoping for, so she views this available male as a 'work-in-progress' - basic raw material with a decent structure, but needing some changes; a project; something she can work with and mold into an acceptable finished product.

Unfortunately, over time, they'll both be disappointed. As you might have guessed, she is the one who changes – much to the amazement of the hapless male. Right before his eyes, she morphs from the defenseless, needy, eyelash-fluttering, submissive waif, into a take-charge household boss – even worse than his mother, because it's a lot harder moving out of the house to get away from this one.

And as you would suspect, he doesn't change at all. All of her efforts are to no avail. Other than the new wardrobe she picked out and talked him into wearing, his maddening traits are now permanent. She's too late. In order for her to have any chance at success, she would have had to start working on him before his eighth or ninth birthday. Now, years later, the patterns are set in stone.

In some rare occasions this constant conflict may not rise to the surface, but deep down in her mind, it's always there, no matter how often he says "yes, dear." She wanted to get married in the worst way, and she did. But don't take this author's word for it. All you have to do is go to any decent dinner restaurant and look at the couples sitting there. Some will be talking to each other and looking like they care about what the other person is saying... and then there are the married couples, just sitting there and looking around, imagining how much greener that grass on the other side must be.

This strange situation has been tremendous fodder for the entertainment industry, as evidenced in television series from the Dick Van Dyke Show, Lucy & Desi and Everyone Loves Raymond, to countless other sitcoms and commercials

The Abridged Female-to-English Dictionary
by Dr. Nick Shoveen, Ph.D.

with a frustrated female who is forced to deal with a bumbling mate. Truly, the line between comedy and tragedy is a fine one.

Hopefully, scientists mapping the human genome will someday find the genes that control desires for shopping, fashion and homemaking, and learn to make them compatible with those that control attraction to sporting events and avoiding meaningful conversation. In the meantime, males will be forced to deal with women who they will never understand, because females feel that the problems are so self-evident, that they don't need explanation. Men just don't get it, and they never will.

This book is designed to help males try to understand what is going on behind the communications they receive. No female in a relationship should ever be expected to be capable of or wanting to take the time to explain exactly what's going on in her mind and how she feels. There are very few people in the world like Doctor Phil, who can actually get in touch with personal feelings and explain them. Too much conversation is in code.

Introduction

If you live in a society where females are allowed to drive cars and aren't punished by stoning, then don't make memorizing the Koran your primary responsibility: this is the book you should know from cover to cover.

> "No one has a finer command of language than the person who keeps her mouth shut."
> *Sam Rayburn*

2

Silence

Innate, inbred talents will often astound the uninitiated. One of these qualities is the female's ability to express more thoughts by saying nothing than by actually speaking. This may have been learned thousands of years ago before humans mastered speech, and for some strange reason, the practice has remained in the female memory bank.

In one particular case we've heard of, an angry wife took out her frustrations by housecleaning. Just a mild disturbance might set off some mild 'dusting' spree.

Silence

Medium frustration could lead to dusting, followed by re-folding laundry. In severe episodes, the vacuum cleaner would be used sometimes for more than a full hour, followed by a period of celibacy.

If you are in a relationship where short periods of silence are accompanied by longer periods of cleaning (other busy-work may be substituted), the first thing to realize is that a fire is burning: if you don't do something to put it out quickly, it will fester into an inferno.

A well-known comedian used to tell what he called his 'jack' story. It was about a fellow who was traveling cross-country, and several minutes after passing a gas station, one of his tires went flat.

Not having a spare tire or jack, he knew that the only way his trip could continue was if he walked about two miles back to the gas station and borrowed a jack, so he could remove his flat tire and roll it back there for repair.

During his walk, the fellow started to mentally recount horror stories he had heard about the way that out-of-the-way gas stations had gouged distressed

The Abridged Female-to-English Dictionary
by Dr. Nick Shoveen, Ph.D.

motorists. In his mind, he was creating a series of worst-case scenarios that angered him towards gas station operators worldwide. His imagination affected his behavior to such an extent, that he actually hated the gas station man before even meeting him.

By this time his feeling was so intense, it overwhelmed the confused driver. He finally reached the station and the friendly manager walked over to him, smiling, with his hand outstretched, saying "howdy, friend, what can I do for you today?"

Unfortunately, it was too late. The driver looked at the gas station man, sneered, and turning away in anger to walk away said, "take the damn jack and stick it up your ass!"

Fortunately (or unfortunately, as the case may be), a comedian's joke isn't required to have a sensible ending, so the audiences usually will just laugh, instead of asking "how did he ever get to fix his tire?" Unfortunately, real life needs some sort of sensibility, so if you find yourself sitting in your residence while your female is feverishly vacuuming, you should be prepared to take some action to interrupt her building up that 'jack' story in her head (insert your name, instead of 'the jack').

Left unattended, her emotions will build as she cleans, so that if you wait too long to try and stop the scenario building in her mind, you may be faced with what the gas station owner encountered – a completely non-sensible ending.

This begs the question of how to interact in a situation like this. Suffice it to say that it would be unwise to attempt humor... she's in no mood for it. Same goes for an erotic advance, flattery, gift offer, or saying the usual stupid thing like, "is something wrong, honey?"

This will only serve to aggravate the situation, because there's obviously something wrong, and the mere fact that you have to ask is further confirmation in her mind that you just 'don't get it.'

A humble suggestion would be to subtly attempt to take her mind off of the subject by switching her over to another 'station.' Some suggestions might be to hit

The Abridged Female-to-English Dictionary
by Dr. Nick Shoveen, Ph.D.

at her weak spots with something like, "I'll be back in a little while..." This can be followed up with a reason for leaving that depending on your knowledge of her, and can be one of the following:

"There's a tremendous sale going on at [insert her favorite store], and I want to see if there's anything there we can use for the house."

Or, "I'm walking down the street. There's a house there just like ours for sale. They're having an open house today, and I'd like to see what they're asking, and how they've got it decorated."

Distractions like these can be dangerous, because they are outright lies. If you intend to try one of them, you should be very careful, because you'll be acting like a dog that likes to chase cars: what would he do if he ever caught one?

Therefore, if the subject-changing line works, you must immediately do another switch, because if she finds out you intentionally misled her, your period of celibacy might be extended.

The second part of the double-switch is a delaying tactic, to allow a brief cooling-off period. If she actually takes the bait and starts to ask about the department store sale or house down the street, you're half way there. Next step is to suggest that she leave the vacuuming chores behind because it's about time you hired someone to come in and do that grunt work. This should be immediately followed by an invitation for her to join you to check out the 'distraction' event, but first, because you're really hungry, you must suggest that the two of you stop off for a quick bite to eat – making sure to mention that you feel like going to her favorite restaurant, because you really have a taste for a certain dish there. It would also be nice to know her favorite dish, so that's what you could have 'taste' for. If she doesn't have any favorite restaurant, you can use a really nice restaurant that you know she's heard of. If you're not too sure what defines a 'nice' eating establishment, one hint is that it does not have a napkin dispenser on the table. Depending on your budget, you can also opt for a place with cloth napkins and a rug on the floor.

The Abridged Female-to-English Dictionary
by Dr. Nick Shoveen, Ph.D.

If this plan works, by the time that the eating (and perhaps some wine) is over, you're half way home. Once you get to the mall, or to where the open house was supposed to have been, it should be easy enough to get her to believe that you may have been mistaken about the date and time of the event, and that now might be a good time to catch a movie.

<u>Caution</u>: It's important to never, ever suggest any action film. If you don't think you can survive a chick-flick, at least have something intelligent in mind – and it wouldn't hurt if it had some graphic sex scenes, because there's nothing like finishing the job by getting her in the mood to completely abandon any thought of celibacy.

This situation has just cost you some money. Not only did you drop from fifty to one hundred bucks on the eating, drinking, movie and popcorn, but now you have to follow up by hiring a housekeeper. The only way partially out of it is to ask her to help you in finding a competent cleaning lady – one who will do a job that she will be happy with.

Silence

There's always a possibility that she may re-think the now defused situation, and let you have a pass on the cleaning lady.

Compared to the spoken word, translating silence is almost impossible. There are only two ways to really find out what brought it about: one is to hire a female private investigator to interrogate you as to exactly what you did and said for at least six hours prior to the silence.

The other way is deploy a secret agent – one of her girlfriends.

If you've been smart, you've learned to become friendly with at least one of her close friends... close enough to call upon her to help you select a surprise gift for your lady. There's no problem creating the occasion, because anniversaries are very romantic, and they don't have to commemorate a wedding. A first date, a first kiss, a first whatever, a 'special' event that you don't want to divulge, etc., etc. They love this stuff, so you'll get all the cooperation you need, but be careful about the budget. A safe way would be to restrict the gift to a certain 'color,'

The Abridged Female-to-English Dictionary
by Dr. Nick Shoveen, Ph.D.

intimating that the hue will bring back favorable memories.

Now comes the foreign intrigue. These women speak to each other quite frequently, so you'll have to question your woman's health. This will get her friend's attention, and you'll have to tell her the symptom – irritability. Your expression of deep concern may create a conversation that could reveal what brought the cleaning episode about. At this point, you've got nothing to lose.

The worst thing that could happen is that the friend betrays your trust, and then your lady finds out that you care about her feelings and wanted to buy her a gift.

And as for the gift, unless you're really out of touch, you should know what color her eyes are. Anything that color will do – and also provide you with a quasi-romantic reason for gifting her: "it goes with your eyes."

And speaking of 'eyes,' here is probably the most common non-verbal communication of all:

Silence

<u>FEMALE</u>:
> The 'Eye-Roll'

<u>TRANSLATION</u>:
When used by a pre-teen-aged girl:
> "My God, is it possible for this guy to get any dumber?"

When used by an adult female:
> "My God, is it possible for this guy to get any dumber?"

The more things change, the more they stay the same.

> "One of the lessons of history is that nothing is often a good thing to do, and always a clever thing to say."
>
> *Will Durant*

3

Body Language

Not all silence is bad – just most of it. The <u>Head Toss</u>, when they throw their hair back over their shoulders, is done to show off their neck and attract your attention. This even works for women with short hair, but you will never see it once the relationship is in effect. It's only done as a minor mating ritual, before you're involved.

Another two signs of possible attraction are the Exposed Wrists (while talking), and Showing the Palms of her hands. This may indicate that she is interested in you.

There is no shortage of books on the subject of female body language, but most of them are all related to the dating experience, and like the examples above, merely try to give some indication of how you can tell whether or not your approach might be welcomed. This book concentrates more on the attitudinal signals that a female will use once there is a relationship in place. The cleaning example is one, and another common one is the arm placement.

If the female stands with her hands on her hips, or sits with her arms crossed, while looking directly at you, you might be in trouble. If she is also looking at her wristwatch or tapping her foot, it may be a 'time' thing. Sometimes simply stopping whatever you're doing can solve the problem that she might believe is interrupting her control of you, like your talking on your cell phone or doing something else that might conceivably be distracting you from her. They usually require a lot of attention, which is probably because they realize we really aren't listening to what they say, so we

The Abridged Female-to-English Dictionary
by Dr. Nick Shoveen, Ph.D.

should at least make it look like we are. Making eye contact is good, but be careful, because there may be questions asked.

<u>FEMALE</u>: "Have you heard a word I've said?"

They aren't known for using short sentences, so it's a good possibility that by the time this question gets asked, she's said many, many words. The best thing for you to do is just try to remember or figure out what main thought she's trying to get across to you, and whatever it is, take a chance and mention it, while agreeing with her. An occasional nod can also give an indication that you're listening.

Sometimes, no matter what you do, you're going to get trapped when she says asks you a question about what she was talking about.

This is a tough situation to get out of so I suggest that you immediately try to change the subject with something that might possibly interest her like, "gee, I hate to interrupt you, but I've been thinking: we haven't been to a really nice restaurant in a while. Let's look for some ritzy place, so we can have a romantic dinner out.

It's been said that with some breeds of animals, you must hit them in the head first, to get their attention.

Caution: You should at least make some effort to try and make it look like you're paying attention when she talks to you, or use the subject-changing gambit. If it works, it might possibly avoid the chance that she decides to employ the animal technique described above.

> "A man who has never made a woman angry is a failure in life."
>
> *Christopher Morley*

4

It's all done with Mirrors

There is one item in every household that may exist in several locations (bathroom, bedroom, dressing room, closet) that can lead to devastating results: the full-length mirror. It is very important that if you ever see your woman parading in front of one of them for any reason, you must immediately exit the room, getting as far away as possible until the crisis passes. Failure to do so can lead to a situation making you wish you were never born: the big *'Question.'* [less-than-lethal questions will be discussed later, in other chapters]

The worlds of science, mathematics and crime-solving all have faced their unanswerable questions: Is there life out there? How many decimal points in π (22/7)? Where is Jimmy Hoffa? In the world of relationships, the dreaded question is,

FEMALE:
"Does this dress make my behind look fat?"

TRANSLATION:
"You're in big trouble, sucker. This is a rhetorical question, but I like to see you squirm, trying to figure out an answer that won't get you into serious trouble."

In all the annals of mirror disasters, only three answers to this question have staved off a tragic ending, and you are now about to discover them:

> a) "I would rather that you didn't wear that outfit. It makes your

The Abridged Female-to-English Dictionary
by Dr. Nick Shoveen, Ph.D.

>behind look too attractive, and I don't want other men to fantasize about it."
>
>b) "Jesus W. Christ! I've never seen it look so good before. Can you wear that to bed tonight?"
>
>c) "No, but if you want it to, maybe we can add some padding."

Any one of these bits of misdirection, when used as your exit line [using one of these answers does not eliminate the need for you to get out of the area], can save an entire evening, but that's not all. The true benefit is that after using each one of them in a different situation may completely discourage her from asking the *Question* again. However, they should only be used in the event you're caught completely off guard and haven't been able to execute your pre-planned exit strategy.

<u>A Sad fact of life</u>: As the years pass, her rear end **will** get fatter – and so will your stomach. The real question is:

It's all done with Mirrors

which one of you will find the other's expansion to be a turn-off first?

> "A man's face is his autobiography. A woman's face is her work of fiction."
>
> *Oscar Wilde*

5

Depreciation

The most valuable piece of property in the mind of every woman is not the home you live in: it's the aging skin on her face, and it's constantly on the mind of every female, no matter how young she may be.

Unlike real estate, a woman's face is like a gas-guzzling American car: all it does is depreciate. Every time they look into that makeup mirror, they're searching for new signs of depreciation, wrinkles, crow's feet, blemishes, or more things to waste money on, trying to cure. The cosmetic industry in this country is gigantic, and probably useless. It's not uncommon to see a 'miracle cream' company told by some prosecutorial agency to clean up its unsupported and exaggerated advertising claims of success.

The entertainment industry has created certain ideals for female beauty that are truly unattainable. A well-known editor of the country's most popular women's magazine was interviewed on a television show. The host asked her about the cover girls on her publication: "Where do you find those models? Are there that many women who really look like that?"

To which the editor answered: "My dear, even those women don't look like that."

Outside of Beverly Hills, California, it's almost impossible to 'air-brush' facial features to create artificial beauty, but a week rarely passes without some afternoon talk-show host introducing some plastic surgeon or former patient, singing the praises of cosmetic surgery.

Sooner or later, you may be faced with another dangerous question... one

The Abridged Female-to-English Dictionary
by Dr. Nick Shoveen, Ph.D.

that can sometimes approach the importance of the infamous 'fat behind'

Question:
<u>FEMALE</u>:
"Should I get a face-lift?"

<u>TRANSLATION</u> (There are several ways to interpret this):

a) I'm responding to peer pressure. All the other girls are having it done;
b) My esteem is being lowered by what I see in the mirror. I need help;
c) I'm getting older, and I'm afraid of losing your attention – or you, entirely;
d) We can afford it, so why shouldn't I look better? You're getting a little grayer, and aging gracefully. It's just not fair. You're maturing and I'm aging.

If it isn't about a face-lift, it might be about a boob job, liposuction, dermabrasion, or some other expensive, elective

Depreciation

surgical procedure that may do much more harm than good.

Be careful here, because unlike the fat-ass-in-the-dress, this situation can lead to permanent and, in some cases, disastrous results.

I have never been an advocate of elective surgery, so the answer to this issue is a very personal and touchy one that begs an important question: is the request for advice due strictly to a personal desire to cure a perceived lack of esteem, or is it being caused by things like peer pressure, pure vanity, or fear of aging? Another thing to be considered is the seriousness of the procedure.

In one particular case, a woman in her thirties decided that she would like to have a mole removed from her upper cheek. It was about a quarter-inch in diameter, and she had it for as many years as she could remember.

This can often be just a 'minor' out-patient procedure, and there's probably no reason not to do it. On the other hand, the quest for liposuction can be cured with proper diet and exercise. I don't think it's

The Abridged Female-to-English Dictionary
by Dr. Nick Shoveen, Ph.D.

a good idea to answer this type of question with an immediate negative reaction, because it will cloud the issue.

A much more reasonable response might be to suggest that you both visit at least one or two doctors who specialize in the particular type of procedure in question, and after learning as much about it as possible, ask the doctor to show some 'after' pictures taken not just a month after the surgery, but as long as five years later.

This may give you some information about how temporary the benefits of the procedure really are, and whether or not it must be repeated periodically – and if that's even possible.

Every courthouse usually has a large plaintiff-defendant index that's available to the public, and it might be a good idea for you to do some homework by checking out the doctor in the local defendant index listings to see what some of his less-than-satisfied patients think of his handiwork. Once you've found one or more case numbers, you can check out

Depreciation

the actual legal file/s to see what the allegations against the doctor were.

There's really no good answer to the cosmetic surgery question, other than to be as considerate and honest as possible with your answer, and hope for the best. Sorry, but that's just the way it is.

> "A successful man is one who makes more money than his wife can spend. A successful woman is one who can find such a man."
>
> *Lana Turner*

6

It's Been a Long Time

A friend of mine told me that he recently received a telephone call from his ex-wife. This wouldn't be very much out of the ordinary unless you take into consideration that it's the first time he's heard from her in almost twenty years.

He's the type of guy who can do (and probably has done) almost everything, from graduating with two degrees in engineering, to building houses from the ground up. Their telephone call was brief, but cordial.

FEMALE (paraphrased):
"...I was wondering if we could get together, to see if there's still any chemistry between us."

TRANSLATION:
"I know you're a well-educated, talented, enterprising man who can do almost anything, and have probably become quite successful over the years since we've been apart. Let's get together, because I'd like to get my hands on some of that success."

The above example is a pretty direct approach, but it can usually be done with a little more subtlety. A judge friend of mine told me the three words he really doesn't like to hear: "By the way."

Quite often when he's sitting in chambers between cases, his clerk will buzz him to get permission to send a friend or acquaintance of his back for a visit. Not wanting to appear rude, permission is usually granted, and the visitor will come into chambers for a brief

The Abridged Female-to-English Dictionary
by Dr. Nick Shoveen, Ph.D.

chat. More often than not, just before the visitor leaves, he (or she) will usually end up with... "By the way..." and the sentence will most often be finished with "I got this stupid traffic ticket the other day, and I was wondering..."

The same principle is often used in the 'it's been a long time' phone call.

<u>FEMALE</u> (after about three minutes of inane small talk):

"...anyway, I just thought I'd call to see how you're doing. I finally made the decision to stay single and enjoy life. I remember you said the same thing once, and now I have to agree with you. Oh, *by the way*, remember Laura, that short, fat blonde girl we used to double with? Well, she's having a birthday party... you know, the big four-five, and she said she'd love to see you again. Can I tell her you'll be there?"

TRANSLATION:
"Forget about the party. It's just a ruse for us to be together again, and now that you think I'm no longer interested in getting married, your simple brain should make you believe that I'm safe enough to get involved with again."

These interpretations may sound terrible, but with people over forty it may be quite common. It's only been during the past twenty years or so that women have been allowed the opportunity and drive to better their lifestyles, receiving encouragement to enter the professional fields of law, medicine, law enforcement, etc., etc.

For too long, the glass ceiling kept them from rising above the receptionist level, and it was rare to see females in the boardroom.

This means that if a woman wanted to ride in a nice new, expensive car, go on expensive vacations, enjoy a yacht, or other luxury accommodation, it would usually have to be as the result of either

The Abridged Female-to-English Dictionary
by Dr. Nick Shoveen, Ph.D.

inheritance, or a man's success. There's an old saying that goes something like, "you can take a boy out of the city, but you can't take the city out of the boy."

The saying also can be applied to many attitudes. When the philosophy of riding a man's success coattails has been drummed into generations of women, it's hard to get that philosophy out.

The entertainment industry has helped bring this philosophy to the public, with successful movies like Demi Moore's *GI Jane*, and the numerous long-running television shows like, *ER*, *Police Woman*, legal dramas and CSIs, the public sees that the modern woman can do anything a man can do – and sometimes better. They might someday be taking over the armed forces too. Hope springs eternal.

> "Woman begins by resisting a man's advances and ends up blocking his retreat."
>
> *Oscar Wilde*

7

Dirty Words

The 'R' word can lead to the 'M' word, which (in half of the cases) leads to the 'D' word.

If you're not ready for a relationship, marriage, or divorce, then there are very few choices available to you.

    a) go sign up at your local monastery;

b) don't ever brush your teeth; or,
c) pay attention to this, and learn how to avoid turning fun dating into a 'relationship' – until **you** want it.

If you're just a normal guy, you'll probably prefer c) above, so the following tips will help you out, but only if you can exercise the proper amount of self-control.

When you meet a female you'd like to spend some time with, start by asking her out for an early evening during the week – not on the weekend. This will accomplish several things. First, because it will be an early evening, it means that you won't have to waste too much time if things go poorly.

Second, it will give you some aura of mystique, making her wonder why you chose a weeknight instead of the weekend. And third, by seeing her during the week, it will give you an opportunity to date other females on the weekend, and give you more latitude in selecting another night to see her.

The Abridged Female-to-English Dictionary
by Dr. Nick Shoveen, Ph.D.

One of the worst things you can do is get into the weekend rut. This happens when you see a female on a Saturday night and then ask if you can see her again on another Saturday. Although it can be quite a lot of fun spending these Saturday evenings with her, what happens when you want to take off for a weekend or go see someone else? Once you set that dull precedent of getting together on Saturdays (and it might only take two or three weeks), the die is cast: she will now expect to hear from you about the next Saturday night.

On the other hand, if you start to see her on a weeknight, and then see her on another day of the week next time, you now have the option of switching the night around to any one of the seven days of the week. This will avoid setting a pattern that she will depend on.

After a few dates, she will no doubt know what you do for a living, so in order to have an excuse for the sporadic date setting, you can use the excuse of 'being behind on a schedule.' This fictitious deadline can be something like working on a novel that you're writing... one that you'd rather not talk about until it's completed.

This excuse can be good for as long as six months, if you work it right.

Remember, the worst thing that can happen to you as a single man is having a female expect you to 'check in' periodically. Don't let this happen to you: keep her off balance, to avoid future problems.

> "We cannot really love anybody with whom we never laugh"
>
> *Agnes Repplier*

8

Humor Me

In many of those ridiculous surveys they take about what women are really looking for in a man, just under the requirements of 'Good looks,' 'Money' and 'A good dancer,' you'll usually see a very popular request:

FEMALE:
"I like a guy with a good sense of humor."
TRANSLATION:
"I don't want you to laugh at my jokes... I want to laugh at yours, or at you.

I get enough crap from my boss at work – I don't need any more when I go out on a date. Make me laugh... and when I do something stupid, make light of it, instead of picking on me."

If you don't think this is true, take a look at all the comedy clubs that have sprung up around the country. Aside from the really brilliant comediennes like Ellen Degeneres and a few others, the majority of comics are male. And the common thread in many routines is their terrible experiences with women. Men are bumbling idiots... to be laughed at, as long as they 'know their place' and realize it's funny to be humiliated.

A man can be a brilliant atomic physicist, rocket scientist, or some theoretical mathematician, and I'll still bet you that his wife thinks he's an idiot when it comes to certain things.

I personally know of a woman whose husband is a successful trial attorney. No matter how dramatic his courtroom victory might be that day, in his wife's

The Abridged Female-to-English Dictionary
by Dr. Nick Shoveen, Ph.D.

eyes, the moment he steps into the house he transforms from brilliant to bumbling.

Another instance is of an extremely talented musician who accidentally put laundry detergent into the dishwasher. This mistake might have gone completely un-noticed if his wife didn't walk into the house to find the living room about two feet deep in overflowing suds from the machine. After paying a service to steam clean the carpets, he was forever banned from using the dishwasher. To this day, I still wonder if that mistake was really as accidental as it seemed.

Unfortunately, this may be the type of humor that the women are looking for, because it gives them great material to use when they get together to swap stupid-men stories. And it works the other way too. A guy I know was watching a three-cushion billiard game on cable TV. When his wife came into the room, she looked at the screen for a few minutes, noticing that the table contained only three balls: two white, and one red. She also saw that there were no pockets on the table.

FEMALE:

"There are no pockets on that table"

MALE:

"Yeah, I know. It's a billiard table."

FEMALE:

"Where do the balls go?"

He made numerous calls from the office the next day, and the response was unanimous hilarity. For the next several years, that guy had some great material to use with his friends.

Another friend also had a material-producing experience. His wife called him one day to complain that the new car he had given her several years ago was making strange noises. He urged her to try to drive it home, and that he'd have their mechanic waiting at the house.

When she arrived, the mechanic went out to check the engine. He came back into the house shortly, and called the husband aside.

The Abridged Female-to-English Dictionary
by Dr. Nick Shoveen, Ph.D.

MECHANIC:
 "Sir, there isn't a drop of oil in that car."

MALE (to his wife):
 "Honey, have you had the oil checked recently?"

FEMALE:
"No, why?"

MALE:
 "The mechanic says it's completely out of oil"

FEMALE:
 "Well, are you sure it had some when you gave it to me?"

TRANSLATION:
 This couldn't have been my fault, because I know you're an idiot. I have the car filled with gas each week at the carwash, and the man there never said anything to me about the oil. I'm going to

have to keep a closer watch on you, before you ruin your car too.

As mentioned above, it goes both ways. Several years ago I attended a lecture given by one of this country's most celebrated authors, Ray Bradbury. During his very entertaining presentation, he admitted that the reason he always requested being picked up and driven places is because he never learned to drive.

And the amazing thing about this statement is that it was coming from one of the country's best science fiction writers, who could obviously master huge important things like time and space in his stories, but couldn't learn how to operate an automobile.

Would one be justified in calling him an author/savant?

> "Professional speakers and trainers have long asserted that you can make your mind up about people you meet the first time, within two minutes. Others assert it only takes thirty seconds. They may both be overestimates."
>
> *Malcolm Gladwell*

9

First Impressions

First dates require an entirely separate set of language skills because it is very difficult to translate from an unknown speaker. It's a lot like doing crossword puzzles: you can become comfortable with a particular puzzle editor's style. Timothy Parker of USA Today can be a pushover, but the New York Times' Will Shortz has the ability to destroy you.

Contrary to popular opinion, it's a good idea to avoid the quiet, luxurious dinner house on the first date. There are quite a few large places with no rug on the floor to absorb sound and if you can find one that also has some music blasting, that's okay too.

My reasoning for this choice is simple: in a quiet surrounding, you have no way to get out of an 'ambush' question. In a louder surrounding, you can always feign not hearing the question ask her to repeat it. This
won't get you out of the situation, but at least will give you an extra few seconds to prepare a defensive answer that won't offend your interrogator.

Here are some examples of the trap being set.

<u>FEMALE</u>:

    a) "So, are you seeing anyone in particular?"

    b) "Have you ever thought about getting married again?"

The Abridged Female-to-English Dictionary
by Dr. Nick Shoveen, Ph.D.

    c) "I guess your career doesn't leave you much time for a social life, does it?"

TRANSLATION:
Any one of the above mean "you're in my crosshairs now, and I want to know if this is going to be a walk in the park. Your answer will determine how hard it will be for me to land you."

Females have numerous tools at their disposal, like preparing you a home-cooked meal, flattery, interest in whatever you say, laughing at your jokes, concern about your well-being, pretending to share your interest in music, sports and movies, sexual innuendo, etc., etc. The ambush questions help them plan their strategy.

A lot of people think that buying an expensive car, choosing a career, or buying a home require the most serious planning... but they're wrong. The internal strategy planning of a female on the hunt tops them all.

Depending on your interest in the female, you're walking a tightrope while trying to answer an ambush question... especially if you'd like to see her again. The trick here is to answer the question with a combination of sincerity and wit, so that the attack is deflected, without the female feeling insulted.

A well-known comedian named Dom Irrera has a clever bit he does about saying things to dangerous people, like mobsters. His theory is that you can say anything you want, and direct any insult you feel like, as long as you have the right introductory and closing sentences. He would suggest opening with "with all due respect..." and closing with "...but I don't mean that in a bad way."

Dom insists that if you follow his opening-and-closing rule, you can insert just about anything you want in between. In the female ambush situation, you're also in a dangerous position, so you might want to follow the rule by prefacing your answer with any lame compliment to her alleged intelligence like, "Gee, you must be a mind reader. I was just going to ask you the same question." Or, "If there was

The Abridged Female-to-English Dictionary
by Dr. Nick Shoveen, Ph.D.

someone else I would rather be with tonight, then I wouldn't be here with you."

Responses like these will never really answer her question, and you're going to have to do better, but it will give her the feeling that you're both on the same page – and also will give you a little more time to create an answer that will almost satisfy her curiosity, while still leaving you in the game. Another answer that might give you some more time (and possible piss her off and give her the idea that you're stalling) is: "I'd tell you, but then I'd have to kill you." Here are some suggestions:

Q: "So, are you seeing anyone in particular?"

A: "I'm a one-woman man. If there was anyone else, I wouldn't be here tonight"

Q: "Have you ever thought about getting married again?"

A: "I've thought about it, but first I'd like to be able to figure out what I did wrong the first time, so I could do it right next time"

Q: "I guess your career doesn't leave you much time for a social life, does it?"

A: "Any guy or girl who believes that is just making an excuse for not finding the right person to be with, because anyone who would rather work than be with the 'right' person, is insane."

If she feels the interrogation is going well, she will try to switch from delving into the future, to getting a 'history.' This is very much what the U.S. Senate tries to do during confirmation hearings for Supreme Court appointees. Unlike what stockbrokers will warn you about 'past performance being no guarantee for future success,' women know that men are constant. So don't be surprised if you hear:

FEMALE:
"How long was your last relationship?"
TRANSLATION:
Are you reliable? Can you be depended on for long periods of time, or are you a flash-in-the-pan type?

The Abridged Female-to-English Dictionary
by Dr. Nick Shoveen, Ph.D.

This question and others that will follow are your employment interview. She wants to know if you can be trusted to stick around for the long haul. The best non-specific answer to this question is: "Not as long as I would have liked it to be."

An answer like this is guaranteed to create brainwave activity in any female. She's now starting to believe that you'll hang in there as long as she wants you to.

FEMALE:

"What was the problem? Did she do something wrong?"

TRANSLATION:

"Okay, let's hear it: you think the whole break-up was entirely her fault, and I want to see how much like her I really am. If you don't get this answer right, I may have to move on."

This is a trick question. She has just given you an opening to pour your heart out about how bad your last female was, and how the terrible things she did caused the break-up. The smartest thing you can do here is to take advantage of the opening by turning the tables on her. If you do it right, you'll convince her that she finally may have found Mr. Right.

"Actually, she was very nice. In fact, maybe that's why it's been taking me so long to start dating again... afraid that I could never do that good again, and worried that I might screw up another good relationship."

This will lead to a long conversation about what you may have done wrong. She now believes that you've realized the error of your ways, and that she can be the one to set you on the right path. They love to direct things, and you are now her new project. Just make sure to let her know that you want to take it slow.

These answers will work over ninety percent of the time, and if you really want to get together with her again, you'll probably be guaranteed another date. She wouldn't have asked you these few questions if she weren't interested. They don't like to waste their time on meaningless surveys. Once the dinner is

The Abridged Female-to-English Dictionary
by Dr. Nick Shoveen, Ph.D.

over and the check comes, you might hear:

FEMALE (to the waiter):
"That was delicious, but it was too much. Can I please take this home with me?"
TRANSLATION:
"It was a so-so dinner, but I don't have a live one lined up for tomorrow night, so if nothing better comes along, I'll toss this in the microwave."

If you have no intention of seeing her again, you should be courteous. Let it slip into the conversation that you like to get a new car every two or three years, because you get bored with a car after too long. She will interpret that as a sign you're not dependable for the long haul and will make her realize you're a poor prospect. Spending time with a man is the most important investment a female makes, and if it doesn't look like there's going to be a substantial return on her investment, there will be an adjustment of her portfolio.

First Impressions

> "The key to everything is patience. You get the chicken by hatching the egg, not by smashing it."
>
> *Arnold Glasgow*

10

The Ultimatum Clock

Any male who can see his female whenever he wants to, can sleep over on a weekend if he so desires, and can have the rest of the time to himself, is a happy camper. During the 'investing her time' period, the average female will allow a relationship to continue like this, but only for so long. The only reason to allow it to exist at all is for the ultimate payoff, which will be some form of commitment.

Similar to the government's desire to know how the country's school children are progressing in the education system, females have devised a group of 'tests' to help predict whether or not they will eventually be receiving their expected ROI (return on investment). The tests will be in the form of casual questions, and it is the male's responsibility to interpret the question in such a way as to determine how long it will be until he gets the *Ultimatum* – As the late great attorney Johnny Cochran might have said – "if you don't commit, then it is the road you will hit."

Here are some of the questions, and exactly how to handle each one, thereby making some attempt to figure out how long you have before something more serious kicks in. The first one is about 2 months into the 'relationship:'

FEMALE:
"Don't you think we make a nice couple?"

TRANSLATION:
You're still in good shape. She's just starting to put the two of you together in

The Abridged Female-to-English Dictionary
by Dr. Nick Shoveen, Ph.D.

her mind. If you can keep her happy, you probably will get another six months to a year from this point on.

FEMALE:
"Are you seeing anyone else? I mean, I'm not, so I was wondering if you were."
TRANSLATION:
She wants an exclusive listing on your property. She's not going to see anyone else, and she doesn't want you to either. Be careful here, because the next step will be her wanting the both of you to move in together. Knowing what her next move will be can give you an edge, so that you can start to do some potential problem avoidance in advance. Maybe drop a hint about your business requiring you to start to travel more, or the fact that you'll be renewing the lease on your apartment for another five years, in order to keep the rental rate at a reasonable level.

If you can hold off on the moving in together and go along with the exclusivity, you may have as long as another six months to a year from this point on.

FEMALE:
"You know, we're seeing a lot of each other. Do you enjoy being with me?
TRANSLATION:
Watch out! This is her intro to the two of you living together.

At this point, you're like a guy on the ground crew at the Goodyear blimp base: he grabs onto the line hanging from the airship, and it's pulling him off the ground. Now, his split-second decision is required, to let go of the line and drop to the ground before reaching leg-breaking height, or to be carried away with the blimp to a more-than-likely fatal ending.

The only edge you have here is that you've had some time to prepare for this, so if you don't want to move in with her, then you've got to take the risk of slowing things down, which might mean you lose her completely. One suggestion might be: "Of course I enjoy being with you, but I've been down this road before, and I'm afraid of getting hurt again, so for the time being,

The Abridged Female-to-English Dictionary
by Dr. Nick Shoveen, Ph.D.

it ain't broke, so I'd like to leave it just like it is, and not fix it, while I build some confidence."

This will give her the impression that you are in touch with your vulnerability, and if she pities you like she should, you might get another six months out of the answer. But no matter how long you stall things along, sooner or later you're going to have to make the decision of whether or not to move in with her, and if you do, for God's sake, make sure it's your place you move into. It's always a terrible mess when it ends, and you don't want to be the one who has to make a move before you've had a chance to find some female and residence replacements.

Just remember one thing: if you do move in together, it will be a maximum of six months before you're officially engaged, so start saving for the ring now. And be apprised of the fact that before she moves into your place, she's going to want some assurances that the relationship is going somewhere, so at that point the game is over. You're going to get married.

The Ultimatum Clock

Marriage can be a wonderful thing, but it's a big lifestyle change, so don't rush into anything. And if you don't think you're ready for it, try to let her down as nicely as possible. They talk to their friends, and if you wind up with a really bad rep in the neighborhood, finding your next female victim might be a little harder.

If you get out while the getting is good, then all you have to do is review the first parts of this book. But, if you decide you're going to live together, then a whole new set of language skills is necessary for proper translation, so read on, but be careful to keep this book in a secure place where she won't discover it.

> The great question that has never been answered, and which I have not yet been able to answer, despite my thirty years of research into the feminine soul is: "what does a woman want?"
>
> *Sigmund Freud*

11

<u>Your New Life (what's left of it)</u>

Living together is a whole new thing. Consider this: you have certain likes and dislikes, many of which involve timing. When to get up, when to have each of several meals a day, what kind of food to eat (or restaurants to visit), what television stations to watch, what movies to see, what friends to associate with, where to vacation, when to go to bed, when to have sex, what events to attend, what to wear, when to shave or not shave, etc., etc.

Female-to-English Dictionary by Dr. Nick Shoveen

Maybe you never thought about it before, but these are just a few of the many decisions that you've been making for yourself ever since leaving your parents' home. These things affect just you, but now there's no more 'just you...' there's 'both of you,' and let the negotiations begin.

You may have had some discussions in the past about what restaurants to eat at, or what movies to see together. That was then. This is now, and both of your entire lives must get into sync, because you're going to have to adapt to a schedule. No more napping after work or having a double PB&J sandwich at midnight. Most females like to eat and sleep on a regular basis, and if they're living with you, they'll want you to join them in those activities. The attempt you'll both be making to get your respective lives on the same page 24/7 will give rise to some new translation requirements.

> "Women get nicer presents after an anniversary is overlooked, then they would have gotten, had it been remembered."
>
> *Shoveen*

12

On a Clear Day

FEMALE:

"Do you know what day this is?"

TRANSLATION:

You've blown it again. On this day of the week, month, year, or decade, something must have happened that she wants to commemorate, and you might also want to, if you had the slightest idea of what the hell she's talking about.

This might not be as bad a situation as you would think, because unless you're completely brain dead, it's probably not the day you married her, her birthday, your birthday, a big legal holiday, or something earth-shattering. Nevertheless, once again she's 'gotcha,' with absolutely no clue.

Answering her with something stupid like "No, honey, I don't know what day it is today" is completely unacceptable: you've got to be more creative, and show her that two can play the same game. Turn the tables on her and come back with some dates that she would never believe you remember.

> a) Yes. On this day two years ago, I saw you wearing your hair a new way and fell in love with you all over again;
> b) Yes. On this day last year, you wore a new dress and looked absolutely stunning.

Neither of these two shots in the dark will get you completely off the hook for not remembering what stupid day this is, but the mild flattery will throw her slightly off balance enough to not get mad at you for not remembering. If things work

The Abridged Female-to-English Dictionary
by Dr. Nick Shoveen, Ph.D.

out right, she'll appreciate your 'try' and simply tell you what the day actually means to her. Then it's your opportunity to snap you fingers and say, "Darn! That's what I was going to say, but I didn't think you'd remember it."

This situation is one of the most important reasons to be computer literate, and be able to work with a database that contains every possible date she's ever mentioned to you since the day you met. But don't get your hopes up, because that 'gotcha' game only works one way. If you ever try it on her, she'll just wave it off and pretend like you're nitpicking by bringing up some irrelevant date that really doesn't mean anything. Life is not fair.

> "Always get married early in the morning. That way, if it doesn't work out, you haven't wasted a whole day."
>
> *Mickey Rooney*

13

The WWW (World-Wide-Wait)

When firing a rifle during target practice, the first thing you should do is adjust the sight. What you want to know is whether it should be moved a few clicks one way or another, to hit the target properly. The same rules apply when living with a female. For instance, you should know how long it takes her to get ready. This will help you plan your own preparation time for a night out.

FEMALE:

"Let me change clothes before we go out to dinner. I want to freshen up a bit."

TRANSLATION:

"Start your timer now, because you're going to learn a new definition for the word 'wait.' I'm going to spend whatever time it takes to get myself ready for an evening out."

The terms she used were 'change clothes' and 'freshen up a bit.' This is the minimum amount of primping done before going out, because it doesn't involve the whole process of showering, and whatever else they do in there. By timing her performance, you can start to get some idea of what she means by changing clothes and freshening up. In the future, you can now work backwards, from the time you want to actually arrive at the restaurant, to the time you should suggest it to her.

Remember: the time it takes her is a constant. Don't ever try to change it or tell her to speed it up, because it will

The Abridged Female-to-English Dictionary
by Dr. Nick Shoveen, Ph.D.

throw her off of her game, and that's when they do all sorts of stupid things like getting runs in their hosiery, to making other mistakes that only lengthen the process an unbearable length of time.

A general rule that I believe applies to physics states that matter cannot be created or destroyed.

The same rule applies to the amount of time it takes for a woman to get ready to go out.

Some things are absolutely fixed and unchangeable.

> "There is no sincerer love than the love of food."
>
> *George Bernard Shaw*

14

A Biscuit, a Basket

FEMALE:
"We need some milk"
TRANSLATION:
"There are about one hundred things I want at the supermarket, so bring your checkbook and be prepared to carry lots of bags."

If all she wanted was milk, she would have picked it up on the way home,

A Biscuit, a Basket

but then, she would have had to pay for it. That will never happen while you are alive.

Be prepared to spend at least a C-note at the market while she loads up the cart with everything but what *you* want. And don't ask about some-thing you might see, but don't recognize ever having had around before – she's probably buying it for her mother, girlfriend, or sister.

Caveat: while on your own during the day, don't ever pick up something that you think would look good on any wall in your residence. Walls are their things. Females believe that if it were left up to you, there would be moose-heads and pictures of dogs playing poker hanging in every room.

> "Lots of people want to ride with you in the limo, but what you should want is someone who will take the bus with you when the limo breaks down."
>
> *Oprah Winfrey*

15

Miss Daisy, Driving

FEMALE:

"Can I use your car tomorrow? I have to pick up some things, and my little car is too small."

TRANSLATION:

"My car is dirty, so make sure you get it washed and waxed, and don't bring it back here with the gas tank empty, like it is now."

This is not as bad as it sounds, because The more chances you get to take her car, the better you can keep it maintained; otherwise it will give out about two months after the wedding, and the chances of her paying for a new one are almost as good as they were for her paying for that milk. A pit boss in Las Vegas once described those chances for me: "Slim and none, and Slim's out of town."

Warning: Before giving her your car to drive, you must make sure that there is absolutely nothing anywhere in it that contains hair, fibers, or other trace evidence that might look or smell like it belongs to any other female. That also includes scraps of paper with names and/or telephone numbers. Once she gets into your vehicle, the average female turns into an instant CSI, and will 'process' your car like it's a crime scene, finding anything that can convict you of something.

And you'd better believe this: there will be no trial. This type of conviction is instantaneous, and the sentence meted out can be extremely severe, over the entire remainder of your life together.

> "There's a way of transferring funds that is even faster than electronic banking… it's called marriage."
>
> *James McGavran*

16

The Gift Horse

FEMALE:

"I used your charge account to get you some new flannel shirts for the winter."

TRANSLATION:

"Those things look great to sleep in, and not one of them goes with any of the clothes I made him buy."

Get used to seeing her wear your stuff around the house. They all seem to have one of those cute little-girl-wearing-daddy's-clothes syndromes.

It's much better to let them buy clothes for you that they will wear, because that may keep them putting on your favorite shirt while they do some painting around the residence. This has an upside: if you ever come home some evening and find her wearing nothing but your shirt, underwear and socks, it may be an invitation daring you to retrieve your articles.

Important advice: Don't ever try to reverse this situation. As a rule, the average female is definitely not amused to see her male wearing any article of her clothing... unless it's done solely at her suggestion. Think twice about this one.

> "Misery no longer loves company. Nowadays, it insists on it."
>
> *Russell Baker*

17

The Loneliest Number

FEMALE:

"Is your friend Sheldon seeing anyone?"

TRANSLATION:

"I promised my girlfriend Vicky that I'd fix her up with someone as soon as she got out of rehab, and your friend Sheldon would be perfect. His eyesight isn't so good, he's never been indicted, and he looks desperate."

This situation can go both ways – and they're both bad. There's no way you can ever wind up ahead in one of those fix-up arrangements. The parties either hate each other with a passion, or they fall in lust and wind up getting married. Either way, you'll be losing a friend.

About the only thing you can do is try to warn your friend in advance, because it's a sure thing your female will be calling him to make the arrangements. The best advice for you here is to try and convince your female that it would be nice if they could be alone together on their first date. "After all, it worked for us, didn't it?" You should do everything possible to avoid the deadly 'double-date' situation, which can be pure agony, because your lady will be hanging all over you doing the lovey-dovey routine, trying to show her girlfriend how nice it is to be in a committed relationship.

If your friend Sheldon is as big a dog as you are, then you must know that any

The Abridged Female-to-English Dictionary
by Dr. Nick Shoveen, Ph.D.

fix-up situation he gets into will end in disaster. You can't win. This is a lose-lose mess. If by some strange quirk of fate they get married, then your friend Sheldon will never forgive you.

If they break up, then your wife will blame your friend Sheldon's failure to make her girlfriend happy onto you.

Once again, you lose. About the only way to avoid this is the truth: subtly hint at Sheldon's secret problem: chronic genital herpes works, and so does a past felony conviction, or aversion to success.

> "The most important thing in a relationship between a man and a woman is that one of them must be good at taking orders."
>
> *Unknown*

18

MoveOn.Don't

FEMALE:

"So, what do you have planned for this week-end?"

TRANSLATION:

Be extremely careful here, because if she doesn't have some undesirable task she wants you to do, she wouldn't have asked the question. It's for sure that she doesn't want you to join her while she has lunch with her friends on a Saturday afternoon, because that's when they all sit around and talk about their men.

Worst-case scenario: she wants you for your body... to lift something heavy, like a piece of furniture that one of her girlfriends is trying to move from one apartment to another. If one of her friends isn't moving, then it may be to help pick up an appliance that one of her cheap friends doesn't want to pay some store's delivery charge on.

It really doesn't make a difference what her reason for asking is. The important thing for you to do is realize that there definitely is a reason, and that before answering her question, you must ask something like, "Why, do you have something that needs doing?"

Hopefully, this will throw her off balance, because she is expecting an answer from you that can be completely ignored, while she goes into her pre-prepared presentation on why you should do what she's going to ask you to do.

By asking this question, she must now re-phrase her spiel: she'll be forced to get directly to the point, without having

The Abridged Female-to-English Dictionary
by Dr. Nick Shoveen, Ph.D.

any answer from you as to your plans. This gives you an opportunity to discover what she had planned for you, and also give you some time to think of a way to get out of it.

> "A man must marry only a very pretty woman, in case he should ever want some other man to take her off his hands."
>
> *Sacha Guitry*

19

Walk This Way

FEMALE:

"Are we doing anything next Friday evening?"

TRANSLATION:

"He's getting almost two weeks' notice, so he better not have anything planned that I don't know about, because there's a seminar on basket-weaving that I want him to take me to."

The mere fact that she's asking about your plans means that she's already made some. You know in your heart that she doesn't want you to take her to a tractor-pull, so be prepared for a sales pitch about some chick-oriented crap that will be worse than root canal work. There is really only one way to safely get out of whatever tortuous evening she has planned for you: divert her to another event – one that she cannot refuse attending.

This isn't as hard as it sounds. First, call around to your friends and find out where at least two or three couples will be gathering. It is important that one of the females who will be there is someone who your present female has never met before.

Next, try this line first: "Well, I didn't make any plans without talking to you first, but I was kind of hoping we could get together with some friends of mine over at so-and-so's house."

She will then tell you how much her event means to her, and will try to 'guilt' you into giving up your choice for hers:

The Abridged Female-to-English Dictionary
by Dr. Nick Shoveen, Ph.D.

FEMALE:

"Well, Okay. I really wanted to attend that seminar, because it would mean a lot to me, learning how to do something on those lonely weekend days when you're out with your friends at some sporting event. But I'll be glad to go with you. I want to be with you, so whatever you want is okay with me."

TRANSLATION:

"If you think I really would give up my event for yours, you're out of your frigging mind. Let's see if you'd like to avoid some celibacy by stepping up to the plate now and giving in to my wishes."

Your closing line should be: "Okay. The only reason I really wanted to go is because a girl I used to date may be there, and I wanted to see what she looks like now, but your seminar sounds like it might be interesting. I'll call them to cancel out."

Before your hand even gets to the phone, she'll be convincing you that she really wants to go hang out with your friends next Friday evening. Once she believes that an old girlfriend of yours will be there, there's no way she'll pass up an opportunity to gloat over her victory and see what one of her predecessors looks like.

Now that the plan has worked for you, all you have to do is make sure that the guy who was supposed to be bringing your ex-girlfriend to the party plays along with the game by apologizing for her not being there. It would be frosting on the cake if he would also like to toss in, "I never realized how fat she's gotten over the past couple of years, so I don't feel too bad about her not being able to be here tonight."

That should finish things off nicely. Your female will feel that you now realize that you made the right choice, and you're lucky you wound up with her instead of with the fat chick.

> "I've never been jealous, not even when my dad finished the fifth grade a year before I did."
>
> *Jeff Foxworthy*

20

Curiosity Killed the Cat

FEMALE:

"How many times have you slept with someone for sex, before me?"

TRANSLATION:

She wants to know how she stacks up against the others, but she's too timid to come right out with it. This is a non-lethal question, which means that it will probably lead to some type of minor argument, but it's not necessarily a relationship-ender, if you handle it right.

Never overstate your actual sexual history. A famous basketball player named Wilt Chamberlain wrote a book (*A View From Above*), in which he claimed to have slept with twenty thousand women. My arithmetic may not be what you would call exceptional, but using an abacus, I calculated that by sleeping with two different women each and every day, you could hit the 20,000 mark in 27.4 years. I don't know if Wilt was ever asked the question by any female, and if so, how he would answer it, but I would strongly advise any male to play down, rather than up, the actual number.

Here are some suggestions you might try, depending on the situation:

a) "None. My life began when I met you."
b) "You're the second, since my little sister."
c) "Do the guys I was in prison with count?"
d) "Actually, you're the first. Was it noticeable?"

The Abridged Female-to-English Dictionary
by Dr. Nick Shoveen, Ph.D.

    e) "Why – did I do something wrong? I'll try harder next time, honest."

Of course, none of the above will work, but it will give her a sense of realization that the question is one that's way out of line and shouldn't be asked. Not that this has ever stopped a female from asking it.

One way to handle it is to simply say, "C'mon now. I would never ask you a question like that, so why not let it go with us both realizing that neither of us was a virgin when we met, and that the most important thing about our sex life isn't about the past, but how we make it for the future. I've been around a little, and maybe you have too, but right now, you're the only one for me, and I'd like to think you feel the same."

If that answer doesn't get the job done and she keeps pushing, the best way to go would probably be to say that the number is embarrassingly small, because you never liked to play around too much, and instead prefer being a one-woman

man, just like you are now. Just keep in mind the old adage that 'the truth can set you free' – but sometimes, before you've found somewhere else to stay.

> "The cure for boredom is curiosity. There is no cure for curiosity."
>
> *Ellen Parr*

21

Entrapment

Once your relationship has reached the intimacy stage, in addition to the previous question about your past quantitative history, a female will often come up with another topic to terrorize you with the concern of failing to answer correctly.

FEMALE:
"Have you ever been with a real prostitute?"

or,

"Do you think I'd make a very good hooker?"

TRANSLATION: Either one of these questions reveals a deep-felt lack of esteem. In a similar fashion as the previous question about how many females you've slept with, she isn't so much curious about your relationship with a pro as she is about how her own performance stacks up, in comparison.

Of course your history is important to her, because it's just another piece of the puzzle she's trying to put together about you, but with these questions, the comparison factor is primary.

The first thing you must do is spot the true motivation behind the question, before stumbling into some incoherent attempt at an answer.

But, if you insist on answering, here's one that's worked for other guys in the past, notwithstanding whether or not it speaks the truth:

"I've never done anything like that, and would never consider doing it, for several reasons. First, it's unhealthy. Women like that, no matter how classy they might want you to think they are, can be unwitting carriers of any number of

The Abridged Female-to-English Dictionary
by Dr. Nick Shoveen, Ph.D.

diseases... none of which I'd enjoy having, or bringing with me to someone in the future who I really cared about.

"Second, any female who would sell her body like that, in my mind, is displaying a form of promiscuity that I don't approve of. I'm a one-woman guy, and when I have sex with someone, I like to think it's because she wants to have sex with me, and not that I'm just a customer.

"And, I'd like to think that whatever way a female acts with me during a period of intimacy, it's real, and not just an act. Sincerity is the real turn-on, not just the tricks of their trade that they were taught to use, to substitute for real feelings."

This type of answer satisfies many of her unasked questions by letting her know that you're probably disease-free, and safe to continue being with. It also releases her from any anxiety she may have about not knowing how to perform like a pro, because she now believes that her sincere expression of feelings will mean more to you than some great sexual trick that you actually would probably prefer she learn how to do.

An upside to this answer is that her curiosity might now be further increased so that she comes up with a new question.

FEMALE:
"What kind of great sexual tricks do they use?"

This can be an unexpected opening for you to slip in some suggestion that might work in your favor, if she goes for it.

The important thing here is to answer the question without losing credibility. This has been known to work for others:

MALE:
"Well, I can't speak from actual experience, but some of the guys I went to school with told me that the hookers they were with would like to _____ [insert your own hoped-for preference here]."

Now that she's heard about the trick, you should pay extremely close attention to her reaction, because it may give you a good indication of whether or not she's game to try something like that.

The Abridged Female-to-English Dictionary
by Dr. Nick Shoveen, Ph.D.

The conversation that follows will be an intimate one, and you'll have to use your own instincts and your knowledge of her personality to mold it the way you want it to go.

As for her question about whether or not she might be a good hooker, the simplest and most effective answer to that one is: "I think you're hot, so no matter what you do, it's better than any hooker could be for me."

Just remember: questions like these may appear to be an intelligence-gathering exercise on her part, but in reality they can be extremely informative in their own right. Quite often, by being alert, you can learn more from a female's question than she ever though she could learn from your answer. And using the proper answer can help to mold her mindset to your future advantage.

> "Any American who is prepared to run for President should automatically, by definition, be disqualified from ever doing so."
>
> *Gore Vidal*

22

Outside the Beltway

FEMALE:
"Honey, who do you think we should vote for in the presidential election?"

TRANSLATION:
"I sure hope he has a brain and is for the same person that I am, because I don't think I can last with someone from the other party. I should have qualified him earlier, but it's still not too late to see if he's a keeper."

You can never tell her your true preference, because it's a no-win situation. If you're for the same candidate she's for, you're in danger of being asked to work as a volunteer for the candidate. If you're from the opposite party, then you've got a James Carville versus Mary Matalin situation, and nobody knows how they manage to keep their marriage together.

There is one way to avoid a hassle here (assuming you haven't come out of the closet with your preference for either party previously), and that's to look to her for help: "I don't know what to do, honey. Whoever I vote for usually winds up losing, so I'm afraid to like one of them more than the other. What do you think I should do?"

You've just succeeded in turning the tables on her. Now it's her move to declare herself. She'll probably tell you to vote for the person she wants to lose, and once you agree to do that, the problem goes away.

It really doesn't make any difference, because once you're in the voting booth,

The Abridged Female-to-English Dictionary
by Dr. Nick Shoveen, Ph.D.

you can do whatever you want, and she'll never know the difference.

Important warning: speaking of politics, don't ever get drawn into a discussion about abortion or a woman's right to choice, because with the political polarization as it is nowadays, the topic is bound to come up sooner or later. The only safe way to handle it is to let your female know that your only concern is what she wants, and that you will respect and support any desire of hers – and you think that all men should say the same thing only about their own personal relationship, and not get involved in anyone else's.

When it comes to your relationship, don't concern yourself about politics or religion: do and say whatever it takes to make your own living condition bearable.

> "Curiosity killed the cat, but for a while, I was a suspect."
>
> *Steven Wright*

23

Internal Affairs

FEMALE:

"What does your new secretary look like?"

TRANSLATION:

"If he thinks he's ever going to get something going on the side, he'd better brush up on the Lorain Bobbit story."

Your office is like a great big men's room – no interference from your 'better half' can break through. Sure, she can call every day, but that's not good enough. They want to know that their property will

Internal Affairs

not be 'poached' by some chippie at the reception desk.

Having this knowledge will equip you to deal with questions about people at the office, like marriage/divorce statistics, suspected affairs, and other thinly disguised attempts at intelligence gathering. If you don't handle it properly at the beginning, you'll be in cross-examination hell forever.

Don't try to be clever with this situation by constantly demeaning the office women, because your female will smell a rat if you doth protest too much about those dames at work. A much better course of action would be to try and include your lady in the office culture. Invite her to meet you at the office for lunch. If you're lucky enough to be involved with a female who also has a job, then try to arrange for her to stop by your office after work to meet for dinner. Let her get to know the women in your office.

Once your female gets the observational experience she craves, it'll be easier to feed her whatever misinformation you want. A salesman

The Abridged Female-to-English Dictionary
by Dr. Nick Shoveen, Ph.D.

friend of mine once told me that doctors are the easiest people in the world to sell to, because there are four magic words you can use to get their big heads nodding affirmatively: "As you probably know..." When I thought about it for a while, I saw the genius of his theory. All doctors think they know everything about everything anyway, so if you start with those four words, you've got them on your page and they're already agreeing with whatever sentence you follow up with.

The same principle applies with women. Each one of them firmly believes that by being a woman, she is an expert in all things female. If you want to 'dis' one of the girls at your office, all you have to do is tell your female, "I'm sure you noticed that habit of hers, when she..." Your female will automatically be agreeing, and whatever information you then feed her about how the dame annoys you will be accepted. Threat ended.

If you're not currently involved in a relationship, don't fall into the same trap that a lot of other guys have. That pretty girl sitting behind the receptionist's desk may look good to you now when she smiles at you in the morning, flutters her eyelashes and says hello, but don't expect her to be sitting at a desk looking like that and greeting you in a couple of years when you walk in the front door and say "Honey, I'm home." Once you take them out from behind the desk, they have a tendency to change.

> "The grass may be greener on the other side, but it also might be poisonous."
>
> *Nick Shoveen*

24

The Substitute?

FEMALE:
"If you could sleep with any one of my girlfriends, which would you choose?"

TRANSLATION:
"If any one of those bitches ever flirted with him, I'll have her killed. And if schmucko here is stupid enough to tell me that he'd actually pick one of them, I just might have him added to the killer's contract."

Get something straight right now: every woman on earth is perpetually in direct competition with every other woman on earth, and marriage, engagement or

The Substitute?

any other form of commitment doesn't end this constant battle; it just acts as a further motivation to increase the level of intensity.

This particular question may also be a telling sign of the fear that all woman have, because they know that the only true cure for lack of attention or erectile dysfunction is not the little blue pill Viagra… it's something that's been around since the beginning of time: you don't need a prescription to get it, and it isn't sold over the counter. It's called *Fresh,* and every male alive desires it, whether he admits it to himself or not. That's why Sports Illustrated's most popular issues are their annual T&A swimsuit ones, why Playboy magazine and others of its ilk are so successful, and surely why there are so many terrible, but sexy female actresses working today.

There's a very old saying that men are familiar with, and that women innately sense: "you show me a gorgeous woman, and I'll show you a gorgeous woman that some guy's tired of screwing."

The Abridged Female-to-English Dictionary
by Dr. Nick Shoveen, Ph.D.

That's right: sooner or later, in ninety-nine percent of relationships, sooner or later the honeymoon will be over, and every woman knows about and fears that approaching time.

They also know that when it happens, it's almost impossible to reverse, so they desperately seek to find out when the dead-line will be approaching, by asking a series of what they consider to be discreet questions like this one, or others mentioned in previous chapters of this book.

Your responsibility is to recognize these acts of desperation, and to treat them in as compassionate a way as possible. This effort requires thought and control. For instance, don't have your girly magazine subscriptions sent to the house: use your office, or get a P.O. box in one of those commercial mailing places, like a UPS store.

Other possible moves might be making derogatory comments about some real 'lookers' that you both happen to see on TV or when out in public together. These remarks should focus on some feature the subject female has that is totally different than your female, like extra large breasts, too much makeup, walking like a runway whore, etc., etc. Try to look at it like from your female's viewpoint, and create what you would consider a 'catty' remark.

This process must be conducted in a clinical fashion, because letting your wife or girlfriend catch you looking at one of her girlfriends or another woman like she's 'on the menu' can be more dangerous than trying to take a bite out of a carcass that some hungry lion busy feasting on. The only difference is that the lion will kill you quickly.

That being said, there are several ways to answer this question: good ways and not so good. You have to make a decision on which way to go, depending on the knowledge you have of your female's personality. The one thing you want to avoid is unintentionally pushing any of her buttons.

Here's a selection of possible answers you might want to try:

The Abridged Female-to-English Dictionary
by Dr. Nick Shoveen, Ph.D.

1. "That's a no-brainer: I wouldn't sleep with any of them. If there were one of them I even remotely considered actually taking to bed, then I would have never cut you out of the herd. You're definitely the pick of the litter, and I'm glad I made the choice that I did."
2. "Would you be there too" I wouldn't want to do anything like that unless you were part of it."
3. "Does it have to be one your girlfriends? 'Cause I think Dame Edna is kinda hot.
4. "Being with anyone but you would only be friction – and I want more than that. I'm not interested in just having sex: I want to be with someone I really care about, and I can't get that with anyone but you."

If any of the above answers look a little too mushy or unbelievable, keep in mind that the women really eat this stuff up. Even if they pooh-pooh your answer,

The Substitute?

somewhere in the back of their minds they'll fantasize that it's true, and that you really mean it.

The odds are pretty good that she'll ask you a question like this while you're both in bed. That's when she starts to think about the subject... while you're trying to get some sleep and not paying any attention to her.

Hopefully, it's not on an evening shortly after you've just poked your mistress, so you've still got a little bit of energy left. When this happens, try to find some spot on her face that's not completely buried in some expensive but useless oily, greasy, moisturizer, cold cream, or wrinkle-remover, and plant a nice kiss there. No conversation is necessary.

After that, there's some chance she'll leave you alone for a while so you can get back to sleep. On the other hand, saddle up, pard, because you may be in for the ride of your life.

> "It destroys one's nerves to be amiable everyday to the same human being."
>
> *Benjamin Disraeli*

25

A Blank Slate

FEMALE:
"Honey, what's your favorite color?"
TRANSLATION:
"I'm just curious."

This is probably one of the only safe questions you will ever be asked by a female, because there's usually no hidden agenda behind it. They're on a never-ending quest to know as much about you as they possibly can.

A Blank Slate

Males are always wondering what's on a female's mind. Females know that there's never anything on a male's mind other than sex, dinner, or sports (usually in that order), so instead, they try to gather intelligence about minor details like a favorite color – that will ultimately appear in every gift she gives you for the rest of your life.

The knowledge they gain this way is never wasted, because like everything else they know about you, including every word you've ever said to them, it is stored in their mental terabyte database from where it can be called up at will either for you or against you. Some day they should pass a law requiring females to give a Miranda warning to males before starting any conversation, because for sure, anything (and everything) you say can and will be used against you in all future arguments.

> "Ask not what you can do for your country. Ask what's for lunch."
>
> *Orson Welles*

26

Petty Theft

FEMALE (in the restaurant):
   "I'm really not that hungry"

TRANSLATION:
   You now must order a large dinner complete with appetizers, side dishes and dessert, because once the food is delivered to your table, her appetite will amazingly

re-appear and the several pieces of celery she ordered will not be enough.

They take great delight in stealing food from your plate, right before your eyes. They think it's cute; probably a habit they picked up while sitting next to their fathers at the dinner table when they were little girls. They're still little girls when it comes to many things, so get used to that behavior.

Also, they hesitate to order as much food as they actually would like to consume, because it might give you an indication of what type of appetite they really have. Another tip-off as to the fact that they're getting ready to raid your dinner plate, is when they suggest things that are on the menu. A harmless suggestion like "Ooh, that looks good. I wish I was hungry enough to order it," means that she wants you to order it so that she can enjoy picking it off of your plate.

It's hard to keep up a conversation and maintain eye contact with a person sitting right next to you, so if you're in a

The Abridged Female-to-English Dictionary
by Dr. Nick Shoveen, Ph.D.

restaurant booth, it's quite common for you to sit across the table from your dinner companion. However, if she insists on sitting beside you on the same side of the booth, this is not necessarily a show of affection. She is pre-disposed to picking food off of your plate, and it will be much easier for her to do this while sitting at your side. Food has a tendency to fall off of a fork, when it is being brought from one side of a booth over to the other side.

There's really nothing you can do to put a stop to this type of behavior without putting a strain on the relationship. Suggesting that she order more food will not work. You are fighting an uphill battle, because this trait is etched in stone, and you'll continually be frustrated by failed efforts while trying to change it. Let her continue being the cute little girl she wants to be, stealing food off of daddy's plate.

The one upside of this particular behavioral trait is that she's a food 'picker,' and not prone to gorging herself. In the long run, it means that you will probably not have to worry about her spreading out too much over time. The only thing you should be concerned about is that these food pickers are usually closet eaters. They usually have some secret stash of sweets hidden somewhere.

> "My wife dresses to kill. She cooks the same way."
>
> *Henny Youngman*

27

Have it Your Way

FEMALE:

"Do you like rice?"

TRANSLATION:

"I'm going to show him that I can be a great wife. After he sees how good I can cook, I'll show him my sewing skills too. Hmmmn... better call mom to get some tips."

It's finally happened. She wants to be a homemaker, and you're going to be the number one guinea pig. This has its upsides and its downsides. You'll save a lot of money that the restaurants would have gotten, but you'll now have to suffer through some dinners that will be so bad that they'll make Scottish food seem tasty.

In a commercial eating establishment, complaining about the food is easy, but this is a different scenario, and you'll have to tread very carefully. There are very few females on this planet who have that magic touch with food: no matter what they toss together, it tastes great… but if you take a close look, I'll bet they're all fat. They love to cook, and they love to eat. Take a look at your female. If she's slender, it's a good bet that she can't cook. The first thing to do is let her try making a dinner and see how it comes out. If it tastes good, then she's a keeper – but if you have a tough time not spitting up, there might be a slight problem situation here.

There are several ways to handle this problem situation. If you are a good cook, then you might suggest that cooking is a thing that maybe both of you can

The Abridged Female-to-English Dictionary
by Dr. Nick Shoveen, Ph.D.

enjoy doing together. This may make the food taste a little better until she gets the hang of it herself, but it may also mean that she thinks doing the dishes is also something you would both enjoy doing together.

If you're not so good in the cooking department, then you might try suggesting that the both of you take some gourmet cooking classes together. Remember this: you can't spend the rest of your life taking her out to dinner every night, so face it: she will be cooking.

I once heard of a fellow who used his female's pet cat as a food taster. Cats have an uncanny sense of smell and unlike the average male, are finicky eaters and will rarely go for something that is not good.

He would wait for the cat to come near the table, and slip a scrap of the suspect dish down to the floor. If the cat ate it, then he would. If the cat gave it a pass, he would try to ditch the portion of that particular item when she wasn't looking. She never guessed why their household used up so many little plastic sandwich baggies.

Here's a helpful Tip: don't try this with a dog, or any other animal, because some of them are just like you... they'll eat just about anything that's put in front of them.

> "Without travel, I would have wound up an ignorant little white Southern female, which was not my idea of a good life."
>
> *Lauren Hutton*

28

Wanderlust

FEMALE:

"My cousin Heather called. They just got back from Europe."

TRANSLATION:

"Everyone's been to Europe but me. He's making a good living, so why can't we go there too?"

It's a given: all women love to travel. They love to get away. I don't know what they want to get away from, because you'll be there too, but they love to travel. Never mind the fact that whenever they get to some exotic location, all they'll do is browse the local shops, women love to travel. Maybe it's merely curiosity about other places, maybe it's just to keep up with her friends by saying that she's been there too. It doesn't make any difference. Women love to travel.

If your female works, try to find out when her next vacation break will be, because she's probably already planning a trip for the two of you. If you're reluctant to ask in advance, try to get a feel for the type of clothing she likes, because that might be a clue as to the culture she's interested in visiting.

I have a male cousin who always wears those brightly colored, obscene, short-sleeved Hawaiian shirts. Hmmm... I wonder what his favorite vacation destination might be.

Traveling alone with your female can be nice if the 'honeymoon' isn't over yet, but otherwise, you might consider talking another couple into joining you. There's a friendly saloon in almost every civilized city, where you and your friend can relax

The Abridged Female-to-English Dictionary
by Dr. Nick Shoveen, Ph.D.

while the girls are shopping. Another benefit in having someone else along is that you don't have to trust that expensive camera to some stranger when you want to get your picture taken.

If seasickness isn't a problem with either of you, a cruise might be nice. Depending on what part of the country you live in, there should be a coast or great lake within one or two air hours away: women like the activities aboard those big liners. And, depending on what your business is, you can check the Internet to find some related seminar going on near your destination location. Consult your tax expert.

> "Too many people spend money they haven't earned, to buy things they don't want, to impress people they don't like."
>
> *Will Rogers*

29

It's on Sale

FEMALE:
"Is that place Pollo Meshuga, over on Washington Boulevard, a good Mexican Restaurant?"

TRANSLATION:
Much like traveling, women also like to save money. Even if they've got millions in the bank, they still desperately seek out bargains. Merchants have known this for years; that's why "SALE" is probably the most popular word in merchandising.

It's On Sale

The female bargain-hunting urge doesn't stop at shopping for clothing or other household accessories that you find useless, it also extends to restaurants, so when she asks if you like a particular eating establishment, it usually means that she saw some advertisement about a 'two-fer' dinner special, a 15% discount, a second 'equal or lesser entrée' for only two dollars, or some other sucker bait to get you in there to eat their crappy food.

My personal experience is that a clean restaurant in a convenient location that offers good food, reasonable pricing and decent service, doesn't need any type of special gimmick to get you in there: their business will grow by word of mouth, or normal advertising about their offerings.

In addition to that, I've always been influenced by one of my uncles, who used to say that he couldn't afford anything that was offered for free, because it always wound up costing him more, in the long run.

The best advice I can give you is, whenever someone offers you something

The Abridged Female-to-English Dictionary
by Dr. Nick Shoveen, Ph.D.

for free, put on your running shoes and get the hell away from them.

> "Health food makes me sick."
> *Calvin Trillin*

30

You Are What You Eat

FEMALE:
"How's your cholesterol?"

TRANSLATION:
"Whatever may be wrong with you now is completely your fault. But, by obediently following my instructions and changing your lifestyle to comply with something I saw on Oprah's show, you have a good chance of being completely rehabilitated."

Good health is a good thing, and every guy should have periodic check-ups to find out if his cholesterol, HDL/LDL, PSA levels, blood pressure, and other indicators are in the acceptable range. But **never** give your female even a tiny indication that one of these numbers is slightly out of whack.

I know of one female, who upon hearing her boyfriend accidentally let slip out that his cholesterol was a little high, put him on a strict diet that included a breakfast of some terribly dry organic cereal that looked and tasted like oxen droppings. He couldn't believe that a food designed for humans could be so tasteless until he read a caption on the box's cover, boldly proclaiming that it was "The best-selling cereal in the UK..." Wow. What an endorsement... a best-selling food item from a country that's completely lacking any taste buds.

> "Health is like money; we never have a true idea of its value until we lose it."
>
> *Josh Billings*

31

The Bug

FEMALE:
"My doctor always expects me to come in once a year for a complete physical exam. What an inconvenience that is. How about yours?"

TRANSLATION:
"If you've got any diseases, I want to know now. You're definitely not worth Herpes or HIV. And, if you ain't gonna to be around for the long haul, because of high blood pressure or diabetes, I'm outa here."

The Bug

That's right guys: it's not enough for you to have good looks, money, a career, dancing skills and a sense of humor, because their long application forms also take your physical condition into consideration. If you've ever heard that applying for a security clearance could be tough, you don't know how easy that really is compared to the mental paperwork that a typical female must go through in her busy mind while she's qualifying you to fill the position of a prospective mate/meal ticket.

Not only do they want to make sure you'll be around for a while, they don't want to be worried about taking care of you or seeing your money spent on health problems. They have better plans for that dough.

Another thing they're worried about is having a sick husband who can't take them on vacations, because as you already know, they all love to travel.

The best way to answer their unasked questions is with a report on your family's philosophy: "My folks have always been great believers in insurance, so a long time ago they took out real big life policies on all of us. I still continue to make all the premium payments on mine,

The Abridged Female-to-English Dictionary
by Dr. Nick Shoveen, Ph.D.

so as long as all of those insurance doctors are satisfied, I guess I'll be around for a while.

This report will satisfy her on more than one level. First, if your parents are still alive, she will think that there's some money coming in down the road, if and when they kick off. Second, she will believe that even if you're not going to be around to grow old with, those proceeds from your policy, along with the past dough from your parents' policies, will keep her and the kids she wants to have, living in a style that she's dreamed of becoming accustomed to.

> "The time to repair the roof is when the sun is shining."
>
> *John F. Kennedy*

32

Tools of the Trade

FEMALE:
"Do we have Philip's screwdriver?"

TRANSLATION:
She's been watching some of those shows on PBS. Having been influenced by the can-do attitudes of Bob Vila and Norm Abram, she wants to do some work around the house now. This cannot be permitted. With the exception of three females that served in the United States Army Motor Pool during World War II, and a large, healthy, gruff-voiced female gym teacher, we once knew, there is almost no

possibility that you have wound up with a lady who can work properly with tools.

This can lead to no good, and will probably make things worse in your residence, requiring professional help from the Butt-crack Repair-it Company, whose serviceman will look at your poor female's handiwork with amazement.

To avoid this hassle, you should tell your female the story about some older women you have met at work, who have permanently damaged fingernails, as the result of improper use of a screwdriver. If this doesn't work, ask her for the benefit of her mechanical skills to help you change the oil in your car next weekend.

> I told my mother-in-law that my house was her house, and she said, "Get the hell off of my property."
>
> *Joan Rivers*

33

Sacrifice Bunt

FEMALE:
"Why don't we have your mother over more often?"

TRANSLATION:
You know that she really dislikes your mother, but now wants to invite her over. This is a ploy. She's willing to endure an evening with your mother, because **her** mother is probably planning on a week-long stay, and the groundwork is now

being laid for what you're supposed to believe is a bi-partisan love-fest.

There is no way to ever avoid her mother's upcoming visit, so you might as well cut right to the core and show your female that there's no sense trying to play this game with you. One approach might be simply to ask, "So when will your mother arrive, and how long will she be staying with us?"

On the other hand, if you still enjoy frequent sex with this female, you might consider a different approach, like "That's a good idea, but it might be better if we had both of our mothers here together, that way their suggestions could cancel each other's out."

Another consideration is whether or not your female is an only child, and what the financial condition of her mother is. If she's an only child and there's a decent inheritance in the works, kiss the old broad's ass every chance you get, and subscribe to the mailing lists at web pages of Rolls Royce, Rolex and Nieman Marcus.

> "My mother says I didn't open my eyes for eight days after I was born, but when I did, the first thing I saw was an engagement ring. I was hooked."
>
> *Elizabeth Taylor*

34

<u>Lord of the Ring</u>

If you're living with a female and are not married to her, whether you know it or not, you're engaged.

Even if you're quite happy with the way things are right now, and have no immediate plans to marry your present roommate, you're engaged.

Even if you haven't discussed marriage with her and have never even thought about buying her a ring, you're engaged.

You may not think you're engaged, but if you could be a fly on the wall wherever your female meets with her girlfriends, you would hear the naked truth: you're engaged.

There's nothing at all wrong with being engaged. I know of one poor chap who was engaged thirteen times (but just married once – to number 9), it's just that *both* parties to the alleged engagement should be aware of the status of their relationship, and agree on it. This is probably the case in about eighty percent of engagements, with at least fifteen percent in which the male doesn't realize he's engaged. Approximately five percent of the time, the female doesn't realize she's engaged. These cases are usually called 'stalking.'

Now that you realize you're engaged, it's time to start thinking about what another comedian says about marriage: "Oh, I get it, we get married, and then you toss me out of my own place and keep all my stuff."

That's a gross generalization of a worst-case scenario, but it's still a remote possibility, unless there's an ironclad 'prenup' in place before the wedding. However,

The Abridged Female-to-English Dictionary
by Dr. Nick Shoveen, Ph.D.

getting a pre-nuptial agreement signed is only a small part of the task: bringing up the subject to your female is the hard part. It is for this reason that I suggest you start well in advance of any talk of marriage. Pre-nups can also apply to people just living together, and that's the way you should approach it. There is no ideal way of bringing up the subject of a pre-nup, but there are a few places where the subject should not be broached: in bed, or at a restaurant. Scenes during either of these activities should be avoided at all costs.

Each state may have it's own set of rules governing pre-nup agreements, but it's generally agreed that each party should have their own attorney look it over before signing, and it shouldn't be shoved under a bride's nose just before the wedding ceremony is set to begin. In an engagement situation, one of these two no-no's isn't relevant, but to make the agreement binding, you should suggest she find her own attorney to look over whatever agreement the two of you want to sign.

Make sure you read the Appendix at the end of this book, for a good primer on Pre-nuptial agreements.

As for bringing up the subject and getting her to go along with it, you must employ a very clever system of reverse psychology: this agreement is for her protection. Even though you may have quite a bit of money and assets, and she's flat broke, you've got to convince her that a pre-nup is good for her.

The best way to do this is by making sure that she has something. I know of one gentleman who worked this plan perfectly, and here is how he suggests you pull it off:

> a) Wait for a special anniversary date, like the first date, first kiss, first whatever;
> b) Go out an buy her a gift that costs at least five hundred to a thousand dollars;
> c) Get the gift presented to her in a nice restaurant.

The Abridged Female-to-English Dictionary
by Dr. Nick Shoveen, Ph.D.

My friend bought his female an expensive diamond necklace, and tipped the restaurant's maitre d' to sneakily walk behind the table, gently placing it around her neck saying, "excuse me madam, I believe this belongs to you." She was then handed a small mirror to see what was placed around her neck.

All the while, my friend just sat there ignoring the whole thing, pretending to read the menu. When she's had a chance to see her prize in the mirror, he winked at her and then said, "happy anniversary, sweetheart."

This scenario, if properly played out, accomplishes more than one thing. First of all, it almost guarantees subsequent sex. Secondly, it reinforces her belief that an engagement is in place, without the necessity of a ring. Thirdly, it endows her with something of value, which sets up the next step.

The male should now express his fear of separation, letting her know that he's afraid that sooner or later she'll tire of him and throw him out. He wants her to know that even if that happens, he wants

Lord of the Ring

this evening's gift, and all the other things he intends to buy for her, to stay in her possession forever... and he wants to put that into writing, for her security.

There will naturally be a round of her denials, pleading with him to believe that she'll never tire of him or toss him out, but sooner or later she can be worn down by his insistence that it will give him piece of mind knowing that she is protected – and that the agreement will also cover a catastrophic parting, like his getting hit by a truck. To make the deal even sweeter, a life insurance policy should be offered, with her being the beneficiary. There's no sense waiting, because the older you get, the more the policy costs.

This last piece of business will surely appeal to the bargain-hunting portion of her psyche, and dissolve all of her other objections. When he finally tells her that having an agreement like that will make him feel much better and more encouraged to take their relationship to the 'next level,' she'll be ready to sign it in blood, if requested.

The Abridged Female-to-English Dictionary
by Dr. Nick Shoveen, Ph.D.

Here are some tips about the agreement itself:

1) Draw up a rough draft on your own, then give it to your attorney to finish up in the proper form;
2) Everything protecting her is to be prominently mentioned in the first part of the agreement;
3) Have the agreement worded so that it applies to the both of you when you are living together, and after you get married.

List the assets you owned before the two of you started living together: you can always tell her that the 'lawyer made you put that in there.'

Any qualified lawyer that the female retains should realize what a touchy subject this type of agreement is, and will no doubt avoid asking a stupid question like, "Are you sure you want to do this?" The reason this question won't be asked, is because if the female backs out, then the lawyer gets no fee, and no sane lawyer would allow this to happen.

Once a final agreement is formalized by the attorneys and signed by the both of you, each party should put it away in some secure place outside of the residence. If you would like to pay for her lawyer fees, make sure that you don't give her the money in advance. You should avoid any appearance of her lawyer working for you. Instead, you may tell her that you insist on reimbursing her for the lawyer's fee, but only after she has paid it.

If she's lacking in funds, there should be no problem with her issuing a check to her lawyer, and you immediately writing one to her, to cover it. You should always maintain different checking accounts prior to marriage, and keep your funds properly separated. This way, you can use your own money to buy things for yourself. If the pre-nup is properly worded, things you buy with your own separate funds should be retained, even after a marriage and divorce.

> "An engagement should come upon a young girl as a surprise, pleasant or unpleasant, as the case may be. It is hardly a matter that she could be allowed to arrange for herself."
>
> *Oscar Wilde*

35

Rules of Engagement

Sooner or later, there will be a wedding. Get used to that fact. It's going to happen. Weddings require a lot of planning. Even if religion doesn't cause an inter-family conflict, many, many, decisions must be made. It's a tremendous amount of work, and being the future groom, you should make every effort to avoid it like the plague.

FEMALE:
"Where would you like us to have our ceremony?"

TRANSLATION:
Your future bride knows each and every detail about this wedding, including where it will be, because she's been planning it since she was five years old. And she isn't the only one who knows exactly what this wedding will be like. All of her girlfriends know about it too, and her entire family has been briefed. You are the last one to learn all of this, and one way or another, she will be using her innate psychological skills to get your agreement to every single aspect of this wedding.

According to tradition, it is the bride's family's responsibility to pay for a majority of the wedding events, with the liquor bill and some other minor things left to the groom's side. If her parents are still available, it would be a very nice gesture for you to offer some financial assistance to them. The offer should be made through your female, because there

The Abridged Female-to-English Dictionary
by Dr. Nick Shoveen, Ph.D.

will be a trade-off: in order to bear the extra expense, you will need more time for your business. This is one way to get out of all the planning.

When you stop to think about it, other than Frasier Crane or his little brother Niles, are there any straight guys on this planet you can name who could possibly care what color the plates, napkins, bed sheets, or any of the other crap will be? There are only two things that mean anything to a man, and they are: having something hot waiting for him on the kitchen table, and in the bedroom. Everything else is window dressing, and it doesn't matter if the male is Archie Bunker or James Bond; if either of these items drops in temperature, it's time to go replacement shopping.

During the entire period between announcement of a wedding date, and the actual wedding, the most important item you will possess is a flask, always full of your favorite alcoholic beverage. It is imperative that you maintain a blood-alcohol level of at least .07 during the entire period of time... feeling good, and still legal to operate a motor vehicle, in most states.

> "There are two dilemmas that rattle the human skull: How do you hang on to someone who won't stay – and how do you get rid of someone who won't go?"
>
> *Danny DeVito (War of the Roses)*

36

Back to Earth

Not all engagements end in marriage: if the male comes down out of the ether in time, he may realize that it's just not the right time to get married, and/or she just isn't the one he wants to spend the next few years of his life with.

This can be a sticky situation, because in some instances, a female has been known to go ballistic when being put on notice that her services are no longer needed. As with the pre-nup, the subject shouldn't be broached in the bedroom – and a public place doesn't work too well either. That leaves one to devise another strategy, and can be exemplified by a well-known old joke that goes something like this:

A college student calls home, and during the conversation, her mother mentions that the daughter's beloved pet cat is dead... it was hit by a car. The daughter is heartbroken. The father, having overheard the mother, criticizes her for breaking the news to their daughter so suddenly. He suggests that she should have started out by saying something like "your cat's up on the roof." Then, during the next week's conversation, "your cat had a slight accident, it fell off the roof and they took it to the hospital." In subsequent calls, the cat's progress could be described as 'serious,' and then 'in 'surgery.' In this manner, when the daughter is finally told that the cat is no more, the daughter would have been prepared for the bad news, and the shock not as bad as in the stark 'obit' in the complained-of conversation.

The Abridged Female-to-English Dictionary
by Dr. Nick Shoveen, Ph.D.

A year or so later, the husband was out of town on a business trip and called his wife. During their conversation, he inquired as to the health of his mother, who had been living with them for a while. The wife answered: "Your mother's up on the roof."

The moral of this joke should be obvious. Don't just clumsily blurt out that the engagement is over. Instead, ease her into it softly, by using a series of comments that might even possibly convince her to break it off as a pre-emptive strike.

If you haven't reached the stage where you're living together, then a simple request like, "Listen, I've lost my job and have to give up my apartment. Is it okay if I move in with you for a couple of months or so, just until I get back on my feet? I need a little time off of work anyway, and maybe in a while I'll look for another job."

This may give her the idea that the gravy train ride is over, and although it may sound terrible, upon hearing requests like this, many females may see their 'happily ever after' slowly sinking into the sunset. They don't want to wind up like the high-school cheerleader who married her football-star boyfriend shortly after graduation, whereupon he took the job he now still has, as a pumper at his father's gas-station.

This isn't to suggest that money is everything, and is even worth more than love, but the ugly, unfortunate truth is that as was mentioned in Chapter III, a female doesn't like to see the possibility of ever having really nice things completely eliminated in advance of the wedding.

Getting back to the 'cat's-on-the-roof' plan, the male must structure the series of announcements in such a way as to avoid giving the female any feeling that whatever happens is her fault. This must be done without ever uttering the words "It's not you, it's me." That would be too clichéd a phrase to use, and because of its overuse, no longer passes the sincerity test. Instead, he should try something like "maybe we can hold off on things for a little while... I'm seeing a doctor about some things. Nothing to worry about, it's

The Abridged Female-to-English Dictionary
by Dr. Nick Shoveen, Ph.D.

an emotional problem I've been dealing with for several years now."

This may give her some idea that you're damaged goods, and she'll now need a week or two to discuss the matter with her posse. Unless you're an extremely wealthy guy (several million, at least), she might decide that you're not worth the trouble, and cut you loose.

If that doesn't work, you've got to come clean and tell her about the insanity that runs in your family, and your fear that it might affect any children you both might have together. Family traits like that have been known to skip a generation or two, so you might consider telling her all about your dear old grandfather, and how he spent his golden years in the asylum, after having deserted your grandmother and leaving her destitute. Destitute is a good word to use. Females don't like that word at all.

Before starting on this course of action, you should visit a shrink. This way, you can stretch out the separation process over a month or so, blaming all your decisions on the doctor's advice. Let him take the heat, but make sure it's a male shrink. You don't want your female to suspect that the shrink is trying to break you two up, just to make her own play for you. Retaining a psychiatrist can cost a few bucks, but over the long run it'll pay for itself in spades.

In rare situations, a female will want you so badly that she'll take all the bull you dish out, and stick with you. If she's a looker, a cooker, and rich, you should rethink your position. She might be a keeper. But, it's a big 'but.'

> "When a guy gets dumped, it's usually because he's either being too nice, too available, too vulnerable and sweet, too predictable or malleable. She therefore loses respect for him and her sexual attraction towards him dies a slow death."
> *Doc Love @ askmen.com*

37

The Party's Over

Sooner or later, all good (and bad) things must come to an end. The best thing you can do is to have some idea of how close that end is, so you can properly prepare.

FEMALE:

"I'm going out with Valerie again tonight. Don't wait up."

TRANSLATION:

Start looking for an apartment, because it's time to leave this sinking ship. Any one of the following situations may now be taking place, listed here in order of probability:

a) Valerie is really some tennis pro named Raul;
b) She'd rather be with Valerie than with you, which is okay, if they'd let you watch;
c) She's really just going to a movie with Valerie;
d) She and Valerie are planning your surprise birthday party
e) She and Raul are planning to use your life insurance policy money.

The best odds-makers in Las Vegas have picked a), so now might be the time to start making some plans. First of all, remove your most important valuables (papers, jewelry, cash, etc.). Think of it this way: if the Court allows you to come back inside for a supervised visit to pick up your things, what would you pick up first? Well, that's what you should now start getting out of there.

Be very careful not to make any removal efforts look conspicuous. When

The Abridged Female-to-English Dictionary
by Dr. Nick Shoveen, Ph.D.

you're told that the end has arrived, you should be able to react to it with a cool indifference, and just walk out with a few things under your arm. Her thinking you couldn't care very much one way or the other, can be important. Sometimes they like to see you destroyed, and you don't want to give that impression, even if it's true.

If you've got half a brain at all, you've arranged for her to move in with you, instead of the other way around. That way, the lease would have been in your name, and it would be her that does the moving. And in the event that you found a place together, and the lease is in both of your names, then don't be so quick to take a walk when she suggests it.

If the two of you have bought a condo, apartment, or home that you're both living in, then call your lawyer immediately.

In one instance, we know of a guy who ran his business out of the house, so everyone agreed that it would be best if he stayed in the house and she moved out.

That way, there would be a steady stream of income that they could both fight over.

CAVEAT: The above suggestions only apply if there are no children involved. If there *are* kids, then consult your shrink, religious advisor, marriage counselor, lawyer, and other qualified people, and completely ignore anything you read in this book.

> ### Quotations from *Rita Rudner*
>
> "Marriages don't last. When I meet a guy, the first question I ask myself is: is this the man I want my children to spend their weekends with?"
>
> "Men who have a pierced ear are better prepared for marriage – they've experienced pain and bought jewelry."
>
> "I love being married. It's so great to find that one special person you want to annoy for the rest of your life."

38

Suggestions for a Better World

My research department has learned that there may be up to 700 Bed Bath & Beyond stores scattered about in the United States, and the average customer occupancy in any one of the BB&B stores is approximately 96% female, 2% male, 1% undeclared, and 1% undecided.

It is therefore this author's educated opinion that the BB&B organization should do the following: install a large screen (at least 60") high-def projection television in each of its stores, advertising that high-profile sporting events will be shown on their screens. Admission for these events should be absolutely free, providing that each male brings his wife.

This will result in men urging their wives to accompany them to a BB&B store, thus creating a win-win situation: the husbands can relax and watch the sporting event, while the wives shop. Additional revenue to the stores will more than offset the loss of display floor space required for installation of the television theater area.

Many heavily traveled roadways now offer special driving lanes reserved

The Abridged Female-to-English Dictionary
by Dr. Nick Shoveen, Ph.D.

exclusively for carpools. Some jurisdictions allow others to use these lanes, including hybrid autos, and other special-purpose vehicles.

A lengthy survey that has questioned thousands of male drivers has resulted in our making a suggestion to the powers that be: a separate lane should be reserved exclusively for Asian and other ethnic minority female drivers. This special lane should be adjacent to the slow lane, so these drivers could utilize every off-ramp, allowing them to repeatedly slow down to a crawl, re-assess their location, and decide whether or not to continue on.

If women are tired of complaining about their men's continual dropping of socks and underwear in other places than the hamper, why not move the hamper to wherever the complained-of droppings are usually left? A more conveniently placed hamper seems like a logical solution to the problem.

Suggestions for a Better World

A national law should be enacted making the act of selling this book to any female a misdemeanor, with a non-disclosure agreement incorporated into any probation agreement.

Never enter an elevator or any other enclosed space in which there is a female attorney wearing an outfit composed mostly of red. If the entire ensemble is all red, then you should quickly get as far away as possible.

The Abridged Female-to-English Dictionary
by Dr. Nick Shoveen, Ph.D.

Never under any circumstances accept this book as a gift from a woman. By the time it gets to you, it's too late. She has no doubt memorized most of it, thereby destroying its usefulness.

APPENDIX

The Pre-Nuptial Agreement

The agreements you read about big Hollywood celebrities signing before they get married have been getting a lot of attention during the past few decades or so, but they're really nothing new. In fact, they've been around for quite some time.

Back in 1786 B.C., King Hammurabi of Babylon created the first known set of written laws, called 'codes,' and one of them set forth the rule that without a contract, no woman of Babylon would be permitted to get married. He was certainly a lawyer's dream come true.

The King's rules about marriage and divorce were quite civilized too: one of them provided that if a woman had no children and had been a 'good wife,' when she split up with her husband, he would return the dowry received from her family, pay her a 'mina' of silver, and send her on her way. That rule might have been the

The Pre-Nuptial Agreement

original idea of the famous saying "good night and good luck."

However, as you may have noticed, a lot of things have changed in the past several thousand years, and just like the lives that we all live nowadays, prenuptial agreements have gotten a little more complicated.

In order to get a better feeling for why it's important to get it right with a pre-nup, perhaps we should look at some examples where things didn't go exactly as planned by one of, if not both of the parties involved.

Famous director Steven Spielberg and his first wife Amy Irving stayed together for about four years, but when they finally split up, the court wouldn't uphold their pre-nup because it was scribbled on a napkin, and she signed it with no legal counsel to advise her.

Fortunately for her, it didn't work out too bad: she is reported to have gotten about 100 million dollars.

Jane Welch was married to Jack, the former top dog at GE. They were together for about 13 years, and their

The Abridged Female-to-English Dictionary
by Dr. Nick Shoveen, Ph.D.

agreement was designed to expire after 10 years of marriage.

They split up three years after the warranty expired, when Jack decided to make an interview he was participating in permanent, by sleeping with the female reporter conducting the interview.

Because actions like that don't go over too well with wives, the lawyers got involved. Jack wound up with a new wife: Jane wound up with about 500 million.

Movie star Ellen Barkin was married to Revlon Billionaire Ron Perelman. When they split up after less than five years of marriage, she wound up with 20 million, but that wasn't the first time that Rich Ron had to spend some money on an ex-wife: he is reported to have shelled out a total of about 118 million to his first three wives.

Lessons learned from the above cases?

   a) make sure that both of you are represented by separate attorneys that don't work for the same firm;

The Pre-Nuptial Agreement

b) don't try to make the agreement cover things that the court will want to supervise, like custody and child support;
c) both of you should sign the papers at least 30 days before the wedding, so there's no last-minute coercion;
d) fairness: don't let an over-aggressive lawyer try to cut one of the parties out with nothing if the marriage goes south;
e) be sure that both of you list all of your assets and debts: get it all out on the table, so there are no surprises down the road.

Other than the standard rules, just about anything goes. Some people have put in clauses that provide some penalties for infidelity and/or excessive weight gain.

There can also be a graduated scale of asset distribution that increases as the years of continuous marriage go on. A clause like that might have avoided the legal battles ex-Playmate Anna Nicole Smith went through when her short-lived marriage to a 90-year-old billionaire ended

The Abridged Female-to-English Dictionary
by Dr. Nick Shoveen, Ph.D.

by his passing away (probably with a smile on his face).

Couples have also tried to specify the rules governing their sexual relationship: others try to set forth the responsibilities of the parties, with respect to who does the chores like laundry, taking out the garbage and other really important things that educated, serious, adult people might like to get straightened out in advance.

Some of the more interesting pre-nup clauses have specified no mother-in-law sleepovers, only one football game per Sunday, mandatory sexual positions, random drug tests, and monetary penalties for rudeness to each other or relatives.

Bottom line: get creative. If nothing else, you can always get written up in the legal journals when the judge says you went too far.

The important thing is not to forget to put in paragraphs that decide the really important things. If you and your intended want to sketch out a rough draft of what an agreement between the two of you

The Pre-Nuptial Agreement

could look like, try to cover these important categories:

1. Indicate both of your names, and include birth dates;
2. Separate Property that each of you now own, and would like to keep, no matter what happens;
3. Future property that either of you would like to remain separate, and not part of the marriage;
4. Present and future property that the both of you want to share jointly;
5. Restrictions on any future claims for Alimony, Spousal Support or Maintenance, in case of a break-up;
6. Full financial disclosure as to all assets and debts presently owned and owed by each party;
7. Allowing for each party to contest the agreement at some future time;
8. Provide for the terms to be binding on successors in interest (other family members, etc.);
9. If any portion of the agreement is found to be unenforceable, it shall not affect remaining portions.

The Abridged Female-to-English Dictionary
by Dr. Nick Shoveen, Ph.D.

Acknowledge that both of you have read the agreement and have had advice of independent, outside counsel (lawyers). And have it notarized.

The above items are just a few of the things that any agreement should contain, but keep in mind that it's always best to have a lawyer involved in the drawing up of a pre-nup.

If there isn't a lot of money to spend on legal bills, there probably aren't a lot of assets to worry about either. One solution might be to use a self-help book to start roughing out an agreement that lawyers can look at and give advice about. If you cover most of the details in advance, that can avoid the attorneys spending too much of their time on the matter, thereby saving you money.

Nolo Press has one that can help you through it step-by-step, so it might be a good idea for you to take a look at it. They have been printing self-help legal books for quite some time now, and can be seen at http://www.nolo.com.

Most states have now adopted some version of the now common 1983 Uniform

Pre-Marital Agreement Act (UPMA), so it's always a good idea to check that out wherever you live, to see what your resident state courts' interpretations of the Act have been over the years.

GLOSSARY

Words & Phrases that she will probably use sooner or later

Maybe… or, I'll think about it…

This may be a common response to any suggestion/s you might make, ranging from what or where to eat, some activity you would like the both of you to do, or anything you can think of that you'd like to do with her that you either have never done before, or haven't done in a long time.

The fact that she doesn't respond with a "yes," but instead uses this word or phrase is an indication that there's no way you're going to get her to go along with your suggestion unless you make it worth her while.

Making it worth her while is a common form of female extortion, during which a brief negotiation period takes place.

It should be noted that their view of negotiation is you giving them whatever they want. The payment usually consists of concessions in future negotiations, during which you would lose out anyway, so you might as well take the easy way out and give in now.

I don't know...

This response is a slight improvement over the 'maybe' or 'I'll think about it' answers because it means there's a possibility of you actually getting your way.

However, a brief period of negotiation will still be required. The upside is that with the 'I don't know answer,' your cost will be a little lower.

Quite often she might use this answer when she really wants to go along with your suggestion. Simply agreeing with whatever you say is sometimes looked at as a waste of assets.

By expressing hesitation, she can get into the negotiation mode. In the

The Abridged Female-to-English Dictionary
by Dr. Nick Shoveen, Ph.D.

alternative, she can simply keep her mouth shut, giving you a brief period of silence, after which you will automatically start in a feeble attempt to sweeten the deal by offering her something she probably would have never thought of asking for to begin with.

As with all other situations, it's a lose-lose deal for you.

Okay, if you really want to...

If you get this response to one of your suggestions or requests, back off immediately! The quicker you admit that it was not such a good idea, the better. If for any stupid reason you actually take her up on this acceptance, the future cost of your apparent success will be too high to pay.

This small victory will be outweighed by having this concession on her part being brought up and thrown in your face every time she comes up with some lame-brained suggestion that you are reluctant to go along with. There's no statute of limitations on this rule. The female memory computer is capable of reaching back an infinite number of years to recall a past concession she may have made.

Caveat: Don't let your withdrawal of the suggestion backfire on you. Quite often she'll sense the opportunity and respond with a direct attack, refusing to accept you dropping the suggestion. She knows that this is a good chance to build up some ammo for a future negotiation. If you let her cajole you into going along with her acceptance, you will pay dearly in the future.

Honey, can we...

This is another danger sign. Any time she starts out a sentence with a nice term of endearment, it means she wants something. What she wants could possibly be something that you want too, but the odds are tremendously against it: she knows what you want and don't want, and she's not going to use up a 'honey' on something that you want too. These sweet words are their ammo, to be saved up and only spent when required, to get the job done.

The Abridged Female-to-English Dictionary
by Dr. Nick Shoveen, Ph.D.

Don't be confused by thinking you can negotiate with her. That's a one-way street. They don't negotiate for what they want. Negotiation and payment is only for when you want something. Females have some birthright to be given whatever they want. This is learned early on as 'daddy's little girl...' and they'll work you the same way they did him.

Yes, I'd love to...

Bingo! You've just struck oil. If you are ever lucky enough to get this reply from a female, you may be on the verge of making a discovery tantamount to the mapping of the human genome.

Well, maybe not the human genome, but at least a small portion of the female brain.

By actually (even only by accident finding out something she'll gladly do without any negotiation or bribery, that's not related to travel or shopping, you may have stumbled onto a small insight into how other males can shape future requests so that they contain some scintilla of the same thing that got her to go along with your suggestion this time.

We are now in the process of putting together funding for the Shoveen Institute of Female Feelings (S.I.F.F.), and one of its hallmarks will be the offering of a sizeable reward for information leading to the discovery of successful ways to suggest that females do things we want them to do.

The small print:

All of the numerous opinions, thoughts, and suggestions presented in this book are those of Doctor Shoveen's and do not necessarily represent those of the publisher Magic Lamp Press, or of his translator, author Gene Grossman.

Any similarity between examples given and real people is purely.

For your further reading pleasure:

Editor Gene Grossman, who helped Doctor Shoveen get this book edited for publication, has also written a number of entertaining novels on his own.

The group of books he created is the *Peter Sharp Legal Mystery series*, and more information about them can be seen at http://www.petersharpbook.com.

The most recent one to be released is ...*Until Proven Innocent* and details of are at http://www.legalmystery.com

About the Author

The very wise and learned Doctor Nick Shoveen, Ph.D. has been offering unsolicited relationship advice to men for many years. Although it has been difficult to verify his entire background, this publisher does know that he claims to have received his Ph.D. from renowned PacoimaUniversity.com, allegedly one of the San Fernando Valley's foremost online schools.

Magic Lamp Press has also learned that prior to his release, the doctor ran a Persian rug concession at the now-defunct Fedco in Van Nuys, California. Well-known yachtsman author Gene Grossman worked for several years translating Doctor Shoveen's pencil-written manuscript from Farsi.

The good doctor currently resides in room 37-a of the Old Bangkok General Medicine House, where he quite often recuperates from serious wounds received in violent feminist attacks, after his public appearances.

Upon his recovery this time, the doctor will continue with his speaking engagements, frequently sponsored by many of the various Gentlemen's Clubs of America, and a hoped-for appearance on the basic cable *Man's Show*.

Watch for him in your town, unless you reside in one of the many cities that have requested the doctor to never return.